DEFYING THE ODDS;

ON THE PURSUIT

OF

SUCCESS

The New Era Of Doing Things

Kamala Thompson

Dedicated to My Mother,

My Family,

My Friends,

Anyone that has ever supported me,

and Anyone that has ever made me smile!

Table of Contents

One Year's worth of questions to ask yourself

1. When was the last time you tried something new?

2. What is your greatest fear?

3. What makes you smile?

4. What makes you lose track of time?

5. When was the last time you did that?

6. Have you done anything lately worth remembering?

7. When you are 75 years old what will matter to you the most?

8. Have you ever regretted something you did not do or say?

9. What has life taught you the most?

10. If you had to teach something, what would you teach?

11. What is the difference between living and existing?

12. Would you break the law to save a loved one?

13. What is success to you?

14. What is the "American Dream" mean to you?

15. Are you successful?

16. What was your biggest dream as a child?

17. What is your biggest dream now?

18. Did it change, if yes, why?

19. If the average human lifespan was 40 years, how would you live your life differently?

20. What do we all have in common, besides our genes, that makes us human?

21. Do you appreciate the things you have?

22. Do you celebrate the things you have?

23. Is it possible to lie without saying a word?

24. If you had a friend who spoke to you the same way you speak to yourself in your head, how long would you be friends?

25. Do you think crying is a sign of weakness or strength?

26. When was the last time you cried?

27. Do you judge people?

28. What would you do differently if people didn't judge you?

29. What do you believe in that most people don't?

30. What life lesion did you learn the hard way?

31. What gets you excited about life?

32. Are you holding onto someone?

33. Are you holding onto something that you need to let go of?

34. Would do you do most?

35. What are you most grateful for?

36. Where do you find your inspiration?

37. When was the last time you felt inspired?

38. Are you more worried about doing things right, or doing the right things?

39. Can you describe yourself in one word?

40. Can you describe your life in a six word sentence?

41. What is the most defining moment of your life thus far?

42. Have you ever been in love?

43. What changed?

44. Whose fault was it?

45. If we learn from our mistakes, why are we so afraid to make them?

46. Is stealing to feed a starving child wrong?

47. What is the most desirable trait another person can have?

48. What can you do today that you couldn't last year?

49. Are you in a better place than you were last year?

50. Would you rather have less work or more work you love doing?

51. When was the last time you lied?

52. What do you wish you spend more time doing five years ago?

53. Who do you sometimes compare yourself to?

54. Who influences you the most?

55. Who is your biggest supporter?

56. If you could choose one mandatory read for all high school students, what book would you choose?

57. Do you ask enough questions or settle which the "norm?"

58. Are you normal?

59. What have you read online recently that inspired you?

60. When do you feel most like yourself?

61. What do you like most about yourself?

62. When you close your eyes what do you see?

63. What personal prisons have you built out of your fears?

64. What are your top five personal values?

65. Why are values important?

66. What is your happiest childhood memory?

67. What makes it so special?

68. When was the last time you touched someone?

69. When was the last time you were touched by someone?

70. Can there be happiness without sadness?

71. Is it more important to be loved or to love?

72. What is the saddest moment of your life?

73. What is the saddest movie you have ever seen?

74.   What gives your life meaning?

75.   What is the difference between falling in love and being in love?

76.   Can there be pleasure without pain?

77.   What does it mean to be a human?

78.   What makes you different from everyone else?

79.   Is there a such thing as over-thinking?

80.   Why do we think of others the most when they're gone?

81.   Who are you thinking about now?

82.   What is the simplest truth you can express in words?

83.   What can you not express with words?

84.   Is there such a thing as perfect?

85.   Who do you admire?

86.   Who do you think stands between you and happiness?

87.   Do you believe in God?

88.   Do you believe in aliens?

89.   What small act of kindness were you once shown that you will never

forget?

90.   Can there be peace without war?

91.   If you looked into the heart of your enemy, what do you think you would

find that is different from what's inside your own heart?

92. What are three moral rules you will never break?

93. When did you develop morals?

94. Why did you develop those morals?

95. How do you know when it's time to continue holding on or time to let go?

96. If I could grant you one wish what would you wish for?

97. How do you deal with someone in a higher position than you?

98. What do you love more than yourself?

99. Who do you love more than yourself?

100. What is your definition of "freedom?"

101. Why are you, you?

102. What do you have that you cannot live without?

103. If your house was set on fire what would you go back in your house for?

104. Do you own things or do things own you?

105. Why must you love someone enough to let them go?

106. Would you rather lose all of your old memories or never be able to make new ones?

107. If you could ask one person, dead or alive, one question, who would you ask and what would you ask?

108. What makes you the most upset?

109. What turns you on?

110. If someone could tell you the exact day and time you are going to die, would you want them to tell you?

111. What would you give up for $1 million in cash?

112. What is one thing you have never told anyone else?

113. What is one thing you have not done but want to?

114. What do you imagine yourself doing in ten years?

115. What is the difference between ignorance and naïve?

116. What is the difference between naïve and innocent?

117. Are you a fake person?

118. Do you know a fake person?

119. What makes them fake?

120. Have you ever been fake to someone?

121. What is the meaning of "peace" to you?

122. Whenever you help someone do you think "What's in it for me?"

123. Would you give up your life to save someone else?

124. Who? Why?

125. What is your number one goal for the next six months?

126. What gets you through every day?

127. If you have the chance to go back in time and change one thing would you do it?

128. What would you change?

129. If a doctor gave you five years to live what would you try to accomplish?

130. What is your favorite song?

131. Why?

132. Who is your favorite artist?

133. Why?

134. Who do you dream about?

135. What is your best skill?

136. What is your biggest weakness?

137. Who do you think of first when you think of 'success?'

138. How do you spend the majority of your free time?

139. Who do you spend time with the most?

140. Why do you matter?

141. Who matters in your life?

142. Can you think of a time when impossible became possible?

143. What is your definition of heaven?

144. What makes you proud?

145. Who are you proud of?

146. How short would your life have to be before you would start living differently today?

147. Is it better to have loved and lost than to never loved at all?

148. How will today matter five years from now?

149. When is love a weakness?

150. When is love a strength?

151. What would the world be like if you were never born?

152. What's your favorite word?

153. What word do you say the most?

154. How much time do you spend on social media every day?

155. Could you spend that time doing something more productive?

156. Why do you go on social medias?

157. When have you worked hard and loved every minute of it?

158. Is the reward worth the risk?

159. Is there ever a time when giving up makes sense?

160. What makes everyone smile?

161. What can money not buy?

162. What is your most prized possession?

163. When does silence convey more meaning than words?

164. Do your thoughts drive you crazy?

165. What song makes you cry?

166. What have you done in the last year that makes you proud?

167. Who is the strongest person you know?

168. If today was the last day of your life what would you want to do?

169. How are you pursuing your dreams right now?

170. What makes today worth living?

171. Do you see to believe or believe to see?

172. How have you changed in that last two years?

173. How many of your friends do you trust with your life?

174. How many family members do you trust with your life?

175. Is blood thicker than water?

176. What makes you beautiful?

177. What word describes the way you have spent the last month of your life?

178. If you left this life tomorrow how would you be remembered?

179. How do you want to be remembered?

180. What are you sure of in your life?

181. What is the next big step you need to take?

182. If you were forced to get rid of everything in your life expect what could fit into a backpack what would you put in it?

183. What would you do if you killed someone?

184. Have you helped someone else recently?

185. What are the three most important components of a happy life?

186. If you could take a single photograph of your life what would it look like?

187. What makes love last?

188. What good comes from suffering?

189. What are you looking forward to today?

190. What are you looking forward to in the upcoming week?

191. Where else would you like to live?

192. Why?

193. What has been distracting you?

194. What was your last major accomplishment?

195. What is your happiest moment?

196. What will you never give up on?

197. Who will you never give up on?

198. What's the best part of growing older?

199. What's the worst part of growing older?

200. What's the best decision you have ever made?

201. What do you think is worth waiting for?

202. What is your earliest childhood memory?

203. What is the biggest lie you once believed to be true?

204. What book has had the greatest influence on your life?

205. What was the last book you read?

206. What is your favorite simple pleasure?

207. What do you fantasize about?

208. What does love feel like?

209. What makes you angry?

210. Why?

211. With the resources you have right now, what can you do to bring yourself closer to your goal?

212. What do you do with the majority of your money?

213. When was the last time you did something illegal?

214. What makes you uncomfortable?

215. When was the last time you felt uncomfortable?

216. What did you do?

217. What is the greatest peer pressure you've ever felt?

218. What will you never do?

219. What is the most valuable lesson you have learned from your parents?

220. Do you want to get married?

221. Are you parents married?

222. What do you see when you look into the future?

223. Why do we idolize sports players?

224. What are your top three priorities?

225. What is your number one priority?

226. What made you smile this week?

227. What motivates you to do your best?

228. When was the last time you lost your temper?

229. How would you describe your past year in one sentence?

230. What would you like to change?

231. What do you do to relieve stress?

232. Through all of life's twists and turns who has been there for you?

233. What three questions do you wish you had the answer to?

234. When was the last time you asked a question?

235. What was it?

236. Did you believe the answer?

237. Who was the last person you lied to?

238. What's been on your mind lately?

239. What do you do to deliberately impress others?

240. What have you done that hurt someone?

241. What has someone done that has hurt you?

242. Did they apologize?

243. Did you apologize?

244. Did you forgive them?

245. Did they forgive you?

246. If you had to move 500000 miles away what is one thing you would miss the most?

247. Who is your mentor?

248. What have you learned from them?

249. What is your favorite sound?

250. What is the best compliment you ever received?

251. What is the nicest thing you said today?

252. What makes you feel secure?

253. What something new you recently learned about yourself?

254. How would you describe your relationship with your mother in one sentence?

255. How would you describe your relationship with you father in one sentence?

256. Whom do you secretly envy?

257. Why?

258. Who depends on you?

259. Who do you depend on?

260. Who would you like to please the most?

261. What is missing in your life?

262. What positive changes have you made recently in your life?

263. What do you want more of in your life?

264. What do you want less of in your life?

265. What makes you weird?

266. What are you uncertain about?

267. What do you think about when you lie awake in bed?

268. Have you ever paid attention to your breathing pattern?

269. What type of person angers you the most?

270. What is the primary quality you look for in a significant other?

271. What's something you don't like to do that you are still really good at?

272. How many hours of television do you watch a week?

273. What do you like most about your job?

274. What do you dislike most about your job?

275. Do you hate anyone?

276. Do you hate anything about yourself?

277. What? Why?

278. What is one responsibility you have that you would like to get rid of?

279. What do you admire about your mother?

280. What do you admire about your father?

281. If you could be someone else for a day who would you be?

282. If you could live forever would you?

283. What is your biggest regret?

284. What are you most excited about today?

285. Who would you like to please the most?

286. How would you spend your ideal day?

287. How would you spend your ideal date?

288. What did life teach you yesterday?

289. Have you ever tried any drugs?

290. Have you every smoked weed?

291. Did you like it?

292. What is the best advice you ever received?

293. Who makes you feel good about yourself?

294. What do they do?

295. Whose life has had the greatest impact on you?

296. If you could relive yesterday what would you do differently?

297. Would you rather your child be less attractive and extremely intelligent or extremely attractive and less intelligent?

298. When you have random free time what do you usually do?

299. Who would you like to forgive?

300. How have you sabotaged yourself in the past five years?

301. What is your most striking physical attribute?

302. When should you reveal a secret that you promised you wouldn't reveal?

303. What have you done that you are not proud of?

304. What white lies do you tell often?

305. What do you do over and over again that you hate doing?

306. In one year how do you think you will be different?

307. Other than money, what have you gained from your current job?

308. Is a college degree important?

309. Do you have a college degree?

310. Do you want a college degree?

311. What can someone do to grab your attention?

312. What makes life easier?

313. What do you love to do?

314. How much money per month is enough for you to live comfortably?

315. How much money do you want to make per month?

316. What could society do without?

317. What could society do better?

318. What makes someone a hero?

319. Do you have a hero?

320. What job would you never do?

321. When did you not speak up when you should have?

322. What are you an expert at?

323. What do you love to practice?

324. What is your favorite place on Earth?

325. Where do you wish you could be right now?

326. What is your favorite quote?

327. Who is your favorite person?

328. How many friends do you talk to regularly?

329. What artistic medium do you use to express yourself?

330. What is the most insensitive thing a person can do?

331. How would an extra $1000 a month change your life?

332. What questions do you often ask yourself?

333. Are you more like your mom or dad?

334. In what way?

335. What is your biggest phobia?

336. What is your favorite smell?

337. Who was the last person you said "I love you" to?

338. Did you mean it?

339. Did they say it back?

340. What is the closest you ever came to dying?

341. What have you lost interest in lately?

342. How do you deal with loneliness and isolation?

343. When did you first realize that life is short?

344. What confuses you?

345. What is your biggest pet peeve?

346. What music do you listen to that pumps you up?

347. What celebrities do you admire?

348. Why?

349. How would you describe your childhood in one word?

350. What are the top three qualities you look for in a friend?

351. What is a specific trait you want to be known for?

352. What is the number one quality that makes someone a good leader?

353. Are you a leader or follower?

354. What is something you wish you did earlier in your life?

355. What is the greatest enemy of mankind?

356. What is your favorite fictional story?

357. Why?

358. What is your favorite time of the year?

359. Why?

360. What is a dream you remember having while asleep?

361. What bad habits do you want to break?

362. When was your first impression of something completely wrong?

363. What was the last thing that made you laugh out loud?

364. What is your first thought when you wake up?

365. If I gave you $1000 right now and told you to spend it today, what would you buy?

What do you want out of life? No seriously, is this something you have ever thought about? As broad of a question it may seem-- it is still one that you should have an answer to. When I think about what I want out of life I seem to digress and think about why I never thought about this at a younger age or why no one around me ever asked me. I want to affect the people around me in a positive way in order to have a spiraling effect. The world needs changes and I would love to contribute to that. On a smaller scale, I have numerous goals and aspirations. Among my friends, for the ladies, most of their life goals consist of marriage, semi-independence, and children and for the guys they want money, hot women, and more money. Maybe it is the estrogen that makes women think more realistic and long-term than guys, but I am not a doctor nor estrogen specialist. On the other hand, all my friends and the people I follow on twitter seem to have this common goal of achieving success in life. If you want to be successful then it is to your benefit to keep reading.

Growing up the only success I ever envisioned was the triumph of dribbling the WNBA official Spalding game ball straight down the paint and jumping right over Lisa Leslie for the game winning dunk. I know, I know, it must have been my estrogen. Unrealistic? Yes, but my idea of success? Yes. Where I am now in my life, about to graduate from one of the most prestigious colleges and start my career, in combination with where I have come from has lead me to dissect what I want success to look like in my life.

I express myself in a bunch of different ways. I will use artistic mediums, but by no means do I consider myself to be artistic or an artist. Being as my schedule can get pretty chaotic, I will use silence as a way to connect to my inner self and listen to what my mind, body, and soul want to convey. On the other hand, I can use meditation as a way to escape my ever-running thoughts.

Every so often, I write down my thoughts in a poetic, sometimes rhyming, way. You know how some people that write poems say that they write as a means to express themselves best? Well, I am one of those people. And since I am the person that truly gets and comprehends what my writing means, I feel like it would not make sense to share with others. So I applaud all artists that understand there are other people out there going through similar circumstances, or have similar feelings and share their art with the world. Still, I had all these thoughts and tips I wanted to share with everyone I know and everyone I do not know, hence the creation of this book. This book is unconventional for a reason. My writing techniques are similar to the spewing faucet of information us students receive from our seemingly unorganized teachers and professors. However, the writing is composed in such a way that you, the reader, are engaged and actively retaining this information I want to share. I am not here to waste your time, grab a pen and paper, a notepad, or your cellphone because you will have to take notes— and sit back and enjoy!

Chapter 2 - What is Success?

A lot of people want to attain success, be successful, surround themselves with successful people, yet have never examined what that actually means. Success in its simplest form is defined by an accomplishment of a goal, aim, or purpose. Hence, you have to have a desired outcome in order to know if you have achieved success or not. As Americans obsessed with the American dream of freedom filled with prosperity and success that leads to an upward social mobility, the idea of success is often how we define our lives. Money, fame, and power are often what we have been told make up success. If we do not get it, we are consumed with envy for those that do get it. Most people will associate success with an accumulation of money or the attainment of profit. However, few people actually develop a detailed desired outcome prior to announcing success. We Americans like to define success by money and what money can buy. We are known around the world as a more materialistic country obsessed with exotic, fancy cars, the size of our homes, and designer clothes. If you can afford those things and still live comfortably do I think there is anything wrong with treating yourself to luxury? No. But if that is it, simply buying expensive things, then we do not contribute to making the world better in some way. Now do not only think on the macro level of famous people and how your favorite celebrities live. Yeah, majority of those wealthy people you are thinking about have many charities and donate lots of money to different charity organizations. But one of the many ways the wealthy avoid paying taxes on their billions is to make charitable donations. When you donate property, you never have to pay income tax on that donation. I am not saying that when you get your first job and your first paycheck that you are obligated to give that to some larger-than-life mission, but I want you to think about how you can contribute to making the world a better place to live in. Think about what you have noticed, experienced, or heard about that made you lose hope in humanity. Think about how you can improve that situation. Do not think that the problem is too large for you to tackle. Think on a smaller scale of how you can help in any way. Helping does not necessarily correlate to donating money, it can be donating your time, or donating your wisdom and thoughts. I went to a meditation center once and the Buddhist monks explained to us that we do not have control over other people's actions and negativity, but we can control how we react to certain things. By having a positive mindset and sharing love for your enemy, compassion, and honesty you will be able to better your life, spread that to those around you, and hopefully have a spiraling effect.

For some, success is defined by effectiveness. Are you achieving your goals? Are you making progress towards your goals? Are these goals contributing to some larger fulfillment? Success for these people means the outcomes become better as a result of their participation. Their contribution is wanted and needed for proper outcomes. They can see the results and feel accomplished by their work, but also know their work fulfills others. In the business world, we see fulfillment as less abstract and more tangible and visible. As a salesperson my goal would be to sell you something and if you buy it that means I was successful. In this example, you had a need for some tangible object and I fulfilled the need, accomplished my goal, and made progress. As a therapist or counselor for someone dealing with depression my goals may be less concise and defined. One goal would be to help the person understand what is causing their depression and give them the proper tools to overcome those problems. Progress in these goals could take more time and the progression would be intangible. Still, these goals would be contributing to the larger fulfillment of filling society with positive, happy, and healthy individuals. For you, being part of something larger in life may give you the meaning and purpose you have been searching for. People that have meaning and purpose in their lives feel more in control and get the most out of what they do. You may find meaning and purpose in your religion, job, or society.

The answer to "What is your meaning and purpose in life?" varies for all of us, but they involve being connected to something bigger than ourselves. People with a calling to do work find their work enjoyable and feel that it makes a valuable contribution to improving the world in some way. These people feel strongly drawn to pursue their work, hence, their work becomes central to their identity. Visiting a meditation center and learning more about the lives of monks and their beliefs forced me to look inward and listen to what is calling me. Some define success by how much joy they have as a result of their work. Work and happiness go hand in hand. These people define success by how they feel when they are working towards their goals and the elation they feel when they have finished. And also by the pleasure others feel as a result of their work. If their work does not add to their sense of happiness and jubilation of themselves and others, then no matter how much money they earn or how many accolades they receive, they do not feel successful. Your job defines your lifestyle and your lifestyle defines your life and your life defines your happiness. Could you imagine having a job that forces your lifestyle to be somber and desolate? Before retirement you will spend thirty plus years working this dull job that forces your attitude towards life to become distressed and melancholy. Our hard working parents and older generations have already fallen victim to countless years of this troubling lifestyle and it is time for a change. Do not fear finding a job that gives you joy. Even though, money does not equal joy, it is possible to make money and be successful doing something you enjoy doing. Business professionals should not go into corporate America because of the monetary gains their expensive suits get. Doctors should not go to work every day because of the six figure checks, but because of the euphoria they feel from helping the lives of others. Teachers should not become teachers for the summers off and same schedules as their children, but for the glee of educating and taking care of the youth of America. How you define success is up to you, but success without happiness seems futile. Others define success by the sense of balance they have between their work lives and the rest of their lives. Here, work is not about success. They believe in balance and that work is not meant to be the only thing in our lives. If a job is driving someone crazy, demanding all their time and gives them no balance between work life and physical life, family time, other relationships, and time for spiritual growth, then the balance is off and many would not consider this as living a successful life. This can lead to a frenetic lifestyle, illness, family problems, and not paying attention to the values that make your life a good one. There are people who feel that they have lost success or not gained it. These people have mental breakdowns, mid-life crises, and get sick just thinking about it. Others give up and decide that success is not all that important; what is important is simply having a job and keeping food on the table. Some at the end of their lives will realize that they never had the success that they thought they had or never actually knew the success they wanted. We can try to avoid issues down the road by defining success. Trying to define success is not an easy task. Success can be an abstract term or it can mean multiple, varying things to different people. Most recognize that in order to be successful and achieve a goal a person most likely has to work hard and believe in whatever actions or paths he or she is taking along the road to success. When someone feels that they have achieved success they tend to be more successful in other projects and other areas of their life. When I asked my friend Chris what success means to him he replied, "Success means being the best at what I do". All my athletes know about this attitude- in sports you do not want to be simply good enough, you want to be the best; come in first place, work the hardest, set new records. My athletes, overachievers, and competitors also know how devastating not being the best and not achieving success can be and how disappointed you become when you do not achieve your goals. Another unfortunate truth about success is the envy it creates. If you are good at what you do, others will look to you and want to be as good as or even better than you, and if they lack talent, skill, or expertise, they will envy you. Instead of people being happy about your achievements, people are fake and hardhearted. In this case it is important not to forget your goals, your purpose and that there are people who appreciate what you have done— the most important person being yourself. Although, your success will unavoidably create envious people, these people will see your success as a means of motivation for achieving their own goals. Most importantly, in the midst of all the hate, is the appreciation and focus you have to promise to yourself. Focus on your positive energy and appreciate where you are now in your life. Do not compare your own life to other people's lives. Unfortunately, too many people measure their own success by comparisons to those around them. If you want to feel accomplished and happy you will have to stop comparing yourself to others. In order to develop your own definition of success you are going to have to stop comparing your definition to the definitions of others. Success is subjective; All individuals have the choice to create his or her own definition of success. Many people have the tendency to compare the low points of their own life to the high points of someone else's. Remember that no matter how perfect somebody's life may seem-- you have no clue what they deal with behind closed doors. Rather than comparing yourself with people who you see as better than you, think about all the people who are homeless, chronically ill, or living impoverished. This will help you appreciate what you have rather than feeling sorry for yourself. No matter how much you achieve in life you will always feel unhappy if you constantly focus on what you do not have. Instead, devote time each day to appreciating the things you do have. Think beyond material objects and appreciate your loved ones, life, and positive memories.

Ultimately, many define success by how their lives will be summed up at their funeral. Will attendees be talking about how much money the person made or will they be talking about this person's contribution and how blessed they feel to have known this person as a friend, family member, classmate, or co-worker? For most, success is ultimately defined by the good that has been contributed and by what is remembered of them.

I am going to guess that your mom or some parental figure told you not to go in the pool right after you ate. You were told to wait at least twenty minutes until your food digested right? And that is exactly what you did. Have you ever tried to go in the pool right after you ate? Did you feel any sickness...or did you feel fine? How would you know what your specific, one-of-a-kind body can and cannot do without trying? Figuring out what works for you does not necessarily mean relying on what works for the majority or average person.

In order to succeed your desire for success should outweigh your fear of failing.

Chapter 3- Being Successful

There are so many distractions that it can be challenging to discipline one's self to accomplish any goals, let alone a monumental goal. By keeping the following advice in mind, you can dramatically increase your chances of becoming successful in whatever you decide to pursue.

Success and preparation are in a relationship of their own. Success loves preparation. If the perfect opportunity presents itself today, would you be ready? It is better to be ready and not have an opportunity, than to have an opportunity and not be ready. To succeed, you must be ready when an opportunity comes knocking on the door. Spend your time preparing for success because when you answer the door you will be dressed and ready to kill. Those who have succeeded know that success is directly and proportionally linked to work ethic. You have to put time in. Because, when you put time in your success will be that much more satisfying. When you are an underdog and do the impossible, it makes success so gratifying and rewarding. Find the purpose and meaning to your life. Start by identifying the things you love to do, things that give you the most satisfaction and things you want to continue to gain gratification from. Consider what subjects you enjoyed in school, and why. This can help give you an idea of what you may be best at or more interested in. Once you identify what you love to do, use this to bond a purpose and objective of your life. Identifying your passions, interests, and values will help you set goals and give your life a sense of meaning. Finding what you love to do will provide you with motivation along the way. If you love animals you will find motivation during those grueling years of veterinary school or if you truly love money you will find motivation during all your failed entrepreneurial plans. Too many of my friends go away to college simply because they have been socialized into thinking that is the necessary next step after high school, without evaluating what it is that they want out of life. How do you figure out a purpose or goal in life? Even though, it is different for everyone and takes a lot of thought and consideration there are several ways you can try to figure it out: Talk with a career coach, or visit of good psychologist- speaking to a psychologist will help you learn extremely valuable things about yourself you never knew existed, don't be ashamed or afraid to visit a school psychologist or an outside counselor, try out several different careers, remembering that even a less-than-fulfilling job can help you learn what you ultimately want to pursue, try making a career out of something you love-- you are more likely to be successful doing something you know you love. Identify the skillsets, knowledge, and materials necessary for you to achieve your objective. This means identifying short term aims to accomplish long term goals. Identify the skills you need to sharpen and the skills you can outsource. Time is one of the most underappreciated aspects of our lives; outsourcing is about time-management. This is called working efficiently smart. Do you think President Obama writes his own speeches? Instead, he has someone else do the writing so he can focus on delivering it right. I work in a commercial brokerage firm where buyers and sellers work smart by hiring an expertise to deliver the services they need. Trusting other people to do their job is necessary. It is hard to be successful if you do not trust the people around you. You will end up constantly micro-managing everything, leaving you spread thin and others bothered about you not giving them an opportunity. Trust in people can be a powerful motivating factor. If you trust someone, they will want to do their best because they want to reward your trust in them. Flashback, to my junior year in college when my basketball team had an entire coaching staff change. Prior to this coaching change it took me two extremely arduous years just to build trust with my first college coaches. Once this trust was developed between me and my head coach everything had changed. I was not only motivated for my own personal rewards, but I was motivated because I wanted to live up to my coach's expectations now that she invested trust in me. We depend on people whether we like it or not, so placing trust in others is a necessity, not an option. Develop an insatiable curiosity. If you do not understand how something works, do not know the definition of a word, or do not know the answer to a question, find out. People often say when you do not know something that you should ask, but how many times has this backfired on you and led you to being perceived as inept or incompetent? Like when you are in class and the teacher says something that does not make sense and you know everyone in the class does not understand, but you are the only that raises their hand, yet you somehow end up looking unwise. Successful people do not necessarily know everything, but they know how to find out the things they do not know. Make the internet your bitch. Do not let Instagram and Twitter make you their bitch. Use all this technology we have in our generation but do not let it use you. Technology can be an extremely powerful tool to connect people, compute algorithms accurately, and ease the burden of mundane data entry tasks, but understand that there are countless ways for people to see things you do not want them to see on the internet. Guidance counselors, parents, and older friends have told you do not post those underage red solo cups on Facebook, Vine six seconds of you shaking your butt, or sext nudies, yet you still have chosen to do so. It is your life and your choices to make, but understand that all choices made on, by, or with the internet, stays on the internet. Being educated gives you the knowledge, skills, and credibility needed to reach your maximum potential. One thing statistics class taught me is that the more education you receive the more money you are likely to make. However, in my opinion, statistics are formed by all of society following the rigid socialization we have been forced into. There is always room for defying the norms. Not all education has to even be formal, apprenticeships and long term training programs are also positively correlated with higher incomes. While focusing on your main purpose, execute your small objective. Try not to find reasons to procrastinate. Break your goals into small steps, and then break it down into even smaller steps. If you have the vision to attack your goal piece by piece, it is easier and less daunting to execute. Make a list of your goals and what step you might take to reach them. Try to think beyond monetary goals, making sure to address both short term and long term goals. Organize your goals by setting a timeline for when you want to achieve specific objectives. Give yourself deadlines that are difficult but doable. I am all for spontaneity and living life to the fullest, but know the difference between living life and having fun from distractions that interfere with you progressing. Stay away from distractions as much as possible. Let me be clear: it is almost impossible to be 100% focused on your task 100% of the time and it is not necessary to be. Balance is key. Distractions are beneficial in low doses, but when your goals start taking a backseat to your distractions it is time to get rid of them. Surround yourself with other people who are successful, have ambitions, or have a desire to reach success in the same way you do. When you surround yourself with people who are highly-driven it is encouraging. You can bounce ideas off one another, network, and they can connect you with other third party networks and resources. Surrounding yourself with driven, successful people is a way to create a culture of success. Change is necessary and even though you may not want to break away from your childhood/hometown friends, it may be what is best for you. This does not mean you cannot have your old with the new, but first you need to make the new friends. You need to look around—who has the success you imagine for yourself? What are they doing? How do they approach life? Do not be shy, ask them for advice. Look to see if you can model some of your approaches around theirs. At school I am always surrounded by success-driven people and it is one of the best motivators I have. My teammates are made up of go-getting college students and have been a support, motivator, and resource in my own endeavors. In comparison, my hometown friends will work mediocre, minimum wage jobs never aspiring to much more whereas my college friends are willing to work for free in a job they know will lead them to a high income career. Although, my high school friends differ to my college friends in socio-economic status, their income should not defer their drive, aspirations, and dreams. Find a mentor, someone with more experience than you, who knows the trade, is willing to offer advice, and helps you in your pursuit towards success. Gather as much information possible. Listen. Study. Research. Understand. Learn. Repeat. Behind many successful people are mentors who have provided inspiration, guidance, and resources. A mentor will help you network; make connections with people who have useful connections, troubleshoot; learn about ways to make resumes, applications, or ideas even better, and strategize; plan different approaches that will help your future. I was fortunate enough to have a database to utilize to locate an alumni who has experience in the real estate field I wanted to go into. Still, finding a mentor was a long process and took some work. I reached out and contacted over twenty alumni, but only gained one mentor. However, my mentor gave me some of the best knowledge on real estate and even recommended me to a commercial real estate firm, where I landed a job. Being a leader not a follower goes a long way. Fortunately, I have always been labeled as a natural leader and I would attribute this to my 'do what I want' mentality. Too often, do I see people compromise their own wants and desires because they just follow the crowd. Even if you are not a natural leader learn to lead in your own way. For example, lead by creating solutions. Question what people around you, in your state, or globally are struggling with or complaining about. Then answer the following: how can I make life easier for them in an effective way? There are social problem solvers like Facebook, technology problem solvers like computer software companies, strategic problem solvers like mathematicians or consultants, and interpersonal problem solvers like psychologists and counselors. A leader stands out by being a visionary and having more foresight than a follower, by having higher grit and tenacity to be able to endure what followers cannot; by having high endurance and ability to accept and embrace failure. An important task of a leader is to establish harmony between the members of the community, which results in the group's maximum potential. To be successful you must be a great unselfish leader. It is easy to be selfish and only concerned with your needs and wants. But, to succeed you have to do what is best for the people; you must bring the best out of those in whom you lead. When you really lead like this, you will really succeed. We focus too much on ourselves and get so caught up in our own desires. If you stop thinking about yourself and concentrate on the contribution you are making to the rest of the world you will lose sight of your own flaws. This will increase your self-confidence and allow you to contribute with maximum efficiency. The more you contribute to the world the more you will be rewarded with personal success and recognition. Take calculated risk and step outside of your comfort zone. One of my teammates always says, "You've got to risk it to get the biscuit." Successful people think big and are not afraid to act big. Do not wait for an opportunity to simply fall in your lap or come to you by luck. Go find them. All investments involve risk and successful people make big investments in their career and in themselves. Study your risks and "may the odds be ever in your favor." Studying your risks involves researching your competition, finding out where you stand, and what your market currently looks like. Be persistent; failure is inevitable, but what will define you is how you carry on after you have failed. If you first attempt did not work, or your first hundred attempts did not work do not quit, do not give up. Giving up is the greatest failure and once you give up you let failure start to define you. Once you have been through hardships, grievances and disappointments, only then will you be able to understand what resilience is. Applying to internships was a long disappointing process for me. Over the course of three months I applied to every real estate internship I could find in New York. I got a few calls backs and emails but nothing seemed promising. Three months later I came home and was ready to quit applying to real estate positions and look for something local. Except, I reached out to my mentor and he recommended I get in contact with a few people. Long story short, I had a series of interviews turn into an internship in the field I was looking for. In my case, persisting with my goal seemed like it would be a failure and waste of time, but ended up working out for me and starting my career in commercial real estate. We must learn from our mistakes. View failures as feedback that provides us with the information we need to learn, grow and succeed. When we view failures as feedback we make the changes needed to be successful in the future. We may be reluctant to try different thing because we are afraid of failing. My motto when going out to eat has always been "stick with what you know is good." Because, how many times have you ordered something new and looked to your left wishing you got what the other person did? Fear of failure does nothing but keep us in our comfort zone. Here we take no risks that might have a high reward. Thankfully, I realized how stagnant and lackluster my food life was. I decided that I wanted to try something different at all my local restaurants. Now, I have been trying all different types of foods from all different ethnicities and not only have I been more than satisfied taste wise, but I have been learning more about different cultures and their different recipes and flavors. When we step out of our comfort zone and try something new, we take a step towards success. The truest failure is not learning from our mistakes. Look carefully at what went wrong, change what you did the first time, and try again by applying the changes you learned. You must take responsibility for your actions. This encompasses responsibility for your thoughts, feelings, words, and actions. Own all the choices you make and the results will follow. Not all of your choices will be the best, still, you have to be willing to take responsibility for your choices. When we take responsibility for our choice, others know they can count on us and we earn their respect. When we take ownership of everything we say and do, we have greater control. Ownership is a whole-life concept; we can take ownership in all areas of our life such as, our fitness, our relationships, and our education. We may not be able to control everything that happens in our lives, but we can definitely control how we respond to what happens. By taking ownership of our actions we create a huge shift in our life. Understand and come to acceptance with the fact that life is not perfect. Accept that life is unfair. Real emotions, sad emotions, doubtful emotions are expected and a necessary part of living and learning, but know when enough is enough. Do not waste excess time thinking about all of the unfairness, instead think how you could use the situation to your benefit. If you complain or whine once in a while, it is not a big deal. However, if it becomes habitual it will be similar to drinking: the more you drink, the stronger your thirst. On your path to success you will see that the successful ones are not complainers. Remove fear and doubt from your way of thinking. Focus on staying positive in every situation—always find the good in the bad. You will be surprised how effective you can be when your thoughts are guiding your actions and not the other way around. If you do fail do not be afraid to start over, be happy that you had the experience and have been given another chance to be even more successful. Dealing with the unfairness of life can teach you the skills necessary to deal with adversity, which is part of the human condition. Fortunately, life is sometimes fair. Generally, effort will determine the outcome. You have an exceptional amount of control over your life and career successes. Life is full of unexpected events and set-backs. This does not mean you are a failure. Often what we view as setbacks are opportunities in disguise. Failure is a single event or experience, whereas success can be an on-going process. Most likely, the more successful the person, the more failures he or she has experienced. If you want to be successful, welcome obstacles. If you do exactly what everyone else does, you will never have a competitive edge. You will always be the same as everyone else. There are countless opportunities out there— try and figure out how to solve a market need. Solving market needs is difficult. However, do not downplay your capabilities because if you think that a problem is too big for you to solve you will wind up with everyone else who did not rise to the challenge. The people who succeed do more than the average person. Sure, there are examples of people who just got lucky—they chose the right parents and inherited wealth or maybe won the lottery, but those chances are slim. You never want to rely on pure luck leading you to success. If you want to stand out from the pack you will need to welcome obstacles, so that you can overcome them. People who succeed at work and in life believe and act humbled by every accomplishment. Well, maybe not every single thing imaginable. But assuming that everything is a gift is a positive way of looking at the problems and appreciating your success in any endeavor. If you do not already admit when you are wrong, then it is time to learn how to accept when something is your fault. This will help you identify what you need to change for the better. Do not make excuses or rationalize your failure by placing the blame on someone else or something else. An excuse after failure is a refusal to make a situation better and will only defer you from growth. Instead, learn from your failure. Do not live with regrets; use your mistakes as education. Each failure is an opportunity to learn because if you make a mistake and refuse to learn odds are you will make the same mistake sometime down the road. Do not waste your precious time making the same mistakes over and over again. Do not rely on the victim card; you have a choice in everything you do. You are not so worthless that you have to keep dating that person that continuously treats you poorly. Obama and the economy are not forcing you to stay in that career you hate. There are other places you could live. And it is not your schedule that prevents you from being healthy. Our social groups are great for complaining. We all discuss our problems with our friends and that is okay. But there are limits. Everyone gets a few opportunities to complain about a particular hardship, but if you seek advice and respond with "but I can't" too many times, you officially become a victim. Eventually, you will have to ask yourself whether you even want to fix the problem. Then, and only then, can you take the actually steps towards fixing or working through the problem. You have to match your behavior with your values. Demonstrate your positive personal values in all you do and say. Be sincere, real, and construct your integrity. Living with integrity means that everything we say and do are true reflections of what we value. Does your behavior clearly show others what you value? Are you depicted as honest and committed or dishonest and indifferent? Are you spending your time with the people and activities you value—or is your focus elsewhere? When we live with integrity we are sincere and true to ourselves. People trust and respect us. These positive feelings from others and within ourselves reinforce our values and build our reputation and self-esteem, leading us to greater success in all areas of our lives. Speak honestly and kindly, think before you speak, and make sure your intentions are positive and your words are sincere. On my college basketball team a lot of the time we have to be critical with each other, sometimes things get heated and harsh words may be used, regardless our intentions are always for the betterment of each other and overall the team.

Words are powerful; they have the power to uplift and enlighten or put down and depress. What we say to others, and ourselves, can have an unexpected, tremendous impact. Speaking with good purpose is about always considering the intention of our words. It is about communicating directly, clearly, honestly, and with a positive purpose. The first step is awareness. If we are aware and think about what we are about to say, we can teach ourselves how to consider the reason behind our words. Negative thoughts are inevitable, but we do not have to say every negative thing we think. There will be times when we need to share critical thoughts with harsh words. At these times, if our purpose and how we phrase our words is considered, the feedback can be very positive, powerful, and build trust. Be willing to do things differently. You have to recognize what is not working and be willing to change in order to achieve your goal. Many times we are faced with situations that turn out differently than what we had originally expected. One way to deal with these situations is to be rigid and continue to do things that same way over and over. Another way (the best way) to deal with these situations is be flexible. Being flexible is responding to changing or new situations in ways to progress us. Simply, if we are trying to achieve something and it is just not working, try another way. Flexibility is about recognizing all kinds of habits or patterns in our life that are not working and bettering them with change, and maybe even changing them again until we find the change that works. If you do not believe in yourself and your abilities, do not be surprised if no one else does. Your negative thoughts about yourself send a signal throughout your surroundings that others pick up on and respond accordingly to. But, when you believe in yourself and your potential, people will pick up that signal and treat you accordingly to how you believe you should be treated. If you know that you look like a confident, capable person, you will start to feel it too. Confidence comes from within; you should dress how you feel best and not what you think confidence looks like. Be careful that you do not overdo it. Dressing appropriately for situations gives you one less worry. Who wants to be that overdressed weirdo at the kid's indoor trampoline party? Carrying yourself with confidence is next. How you carry yourself communicates a lot to other people. Let everyone know how capable, confident, and in-charge you are. Do this by walking with a purpose, standing tall, and looking everyone in the eyes. When you look like a confident person, you will be approached as one. Carrying yourself this way will eventually cue your mind to feel a certain way about yourself. Do not be afraid to smile. You would be surprised by how even the smallest of smiles can make people around you feel comfortable. A fake smile can be spotted from a mile away. So, attempt to genuinely smile more— what is so wrong with happiness? Making eye contact impacts the way people perceive you. It tells people that you respect them, acknowledge their presence, and that you are actually interested in the conversation. By making eye contact you will improve the quality of interactions you will be having, in addition to appearing more confident. Something as simple as making eye contact will make you come off as more likeable, trustworthy, and those who converse with you will feel more appreciated. Overall, establishing an open, confident body language will make you more approachable. If you want others to approach you, you have to be welcoming. As of right now, what is standing in the way of your confidence? Write down all the things that are keeping your from being that confident person you dream of. Everyone struggles with confidence. Some people are good at hiding it, but every person has struggled with his or her self-confidence at one point or another. Confidence is quiet. Work hard in silence; allow your success to speak for itself. Recognize your talents and good qualities, write them down, and pat yourself on the back a little. Focusing on your better qualities will boost your sense of worth. Confidence is not about "dripping swaggu," or a blatant pretense of bravery. Confident people will take a stand not because they think they are always right, but because they are not afraid of voicing their opinion and maybe being wrong. Confident people do not mind being proven wrong. They do not ignore truths or disregard differing opinions or points of views. Finding out what is actually right is a lot more important than being right. Confident people are not afraid to actually listen, rather than speak. Bragging is a mask for insecurity. Confident people already know what they think, but also want to know what you think. We will ask an open-ended question to give other people the freedom to be thoughtful and introspective. Confident people realize they know a lot, yet wish they knew more. The only way to learn more is to listen more. Confidence breeds sincerity and honesty. What are the thousands of Instagram followers really doing for you? Seek approval from the people that really matter in your life. Earning the trust and respect of the few people in your life is more important than getting a bunch of likes on a picture. If you are out of shape you will feel insecure, unattractive, and less energetic. By working out you improve your physical appearance, energize yourself, and accomplish something positive. Having the discipline to work out makes you feel better and it creates a positive momentum that you can build on for the rest of the day. In schools, large gatherings, and offices, people always go to sit at the back of the room. Most people prefer this because they are afraid of being noticed. This reflects a lack of self-confidence. By choosing to sit in the front row you can help yourself conquer this irrational fear and build your self-confidence. During discussions do not be afraid to speak up because you are afraid that people will judge you. In fact, most of the people around you are dealing with this exact same fear. By making an effort to speak up at least once in every group discussion, you will become a better public speaker, more confident in your own thoughts, and recognized as a leader by your peers. Stop comparing yourself with everyone else. Not everything is a competition, and viewing life in that way will unnecessarily stress you out. If you have a strong competitive nature, try competing with yourself by striving to keep getting better. Building confidence is a process—it will not just happen overnight. The process will not always move forward. Embrace your interests, improve your skills, or take up a hobby you have been wanting to try. Do not get discouraged if you are not immediately awesome—learning is a process. Remember that a hobby is supposed to give you small victories or relaxation and recreation time. In order to be confident, you have to do confident things. One of those things will be making conversation with people you do not know. It may be intimidating at first, but after time you will start to get more and more accustomed. Do not over-apologize. Being able to say you are sorry when you have done something wrong, is a good trait. However, knowing when it is necessary to say sorry is something too many people struggle with. Apologizing when you have not done anything wrong makes you subordinate. In some circumstances you can express your sympathy or regret without actually apologizing. Apologizing needlessly makes you seem unsure of yourself and can make you seem inferior to the person you are over-apologizing to. If you apologize all the time, your sorry starts to lose its value. Your "sorry" should be said with care and thought. Did you do anything wrong? Are you really sorry? If not, do not apologize. When someone gives you a compliment, accept it gracefully. Be nice when someone compliments you because it shows your politeness and that you have a secure sense of self-worth. Feel free to go as far as paying a compliment in return. This can help you if you are still uncomfortable taking compliments. Additionally, paying compliments to others brightens their day, making you feel better about yourself, and in return building your confidence. When you become a source of positivity, others will want to be around you and your good vibes. On the flipside, lose those who you feel are constantly judging you. You might be that naturally extroverted, loud, rambunctious person, but the people around you are constantly judging your personality and behaviors. These people need to be ditched immediately. It is important to surround yourself with others who you feel make you feel like you are the best version of yourself. By surrounding yourself with these people you will be able to make the growth you want. Life can be a self-fulfilling prophecy and you need to expect success. Pessimism can undermine your abilities. If you expect success, you might actually just map it out. In order to ensure your financial stability over time learn how to manage your finances—regardless of your level of income. Keep track of your expenses, review your bank statements and notice where you spend your money; keep personal records, and understand your income. Understand the federal, state, and social security taxes that will be deducted from your gross pay and know what your net pay is (the money you end up taking home with you). Prioritize spending with your first priority being your necessities like food, shelter, and clothing. Afterwards, if your income allows, you can spend money on luxuries like expensive clothes, cars, and vacations. Be brutally honest with yourself when differentiating between your basic needs and your luxuries. Do not forget those lump sums you will have to pay monthly for things like your rent and car insurance. Also, plan to save portions of your income every month. You should deposit some of your money into your savings account. Do not be over optimistic and deposit your whole pay check into your savings and disregard the upcoming expenses you will have. You are also going to have to manage your time; procrastinating and putting off important tasks until that last minute can cause unnecessary stress, and increase the likelihood of errors. Manage your time so that you have enough time to complete a task effectively. Quit saying tomorrow because delaying or procrastinating is nonconductive to becoming successful. Us an application on your phone or a paper planner to help keep you organized throughout the day, week, and month. Make a reminder list or a to-do list and check off each task as you complete it. This will help you stay organized and motivated. Crossing or checking something off a task list is a small euphoria of accomplishment that will cause you to want more organization and completion.

Could you imagine dying without living? I cannot. We are born to live and experience life. We are here to make things better for one another. If you are spending your whole life working and not enjoying what you do, you will end up regretting it. If you find yourself constantly bored, daydreaming about the future or past, or counting down the minutes until the day ends it is most likely because you feel disconnected from what you are doing. Consider changing careers or majors to something that you care about. Cherish your time; try spending some of your free time partaking in your hobbies or spending time with loved ones rather than just watching television or on Instagram all day. Not everything you do has to be productive in the conventional sense, but it should be engaging and enjoyable. Remember that success does not guarantee happiness. Avoid making the mistake of thinking accomplishing a certain goal will give you instant gratification. Fulfillment and satisfaction have a lot more to do with how you approach life rather than what you do in it. Do not burn bridges on your way to the top, do not forget to make time for family, friends and other relationships, and always keep your true happiness in perspective. Value experiences over objects. Experiences make us happier than the objects we buy with money. Still, do not be ignorant to the fact that you may need a substantial amount of money to have the experiences you personally want. Focus on making great memories with great people along the way. Enjoy the present moment. Yes, this moment you are in right now—enjoy it! Do not dwell on the past or constantly daydream about the future because you will miss out on what you could be experiencing in that present moment. Remember that the past and the future are simply illusions and that the real life takes place here and now. Start paying attention to the negative thoughts you have so that you can learn to silence them and enjoy your present moment. If a negative thought arises in your head, acknowledge it, label it a negative thought, and then let it fade away. Get in the habit of paying attention to the small details around you. Appreciate the feeling of the sun on your skin, your breathing pattern, or the artwork and landscapes that surround you. Noticing things like these will help you silence a rambling mind and lead you to appreciating every moment. Live purposefully; by paying attention to your actions. Ask yourself, is this what I want to be doing? Is this going to lead me to where I want to be in life? If it is not, then do not do it –

easy enough right. Make the most of every moment. Focus your attention on the present moment and keep a positive mindset. Life is full of opportunities to do something else, something other than what we are doing now. Many of us spend a lot of time thinking about those other things, instead of making the most out of what we are doing now— your focus should be the now. Whenever our thoughts are occupied with something other than what we are doing now, we miss out on what is taking place around us in that moment. While we are waiting for the next moment to arrive, the present moment slips away. But when we live in the now, we have the power. Live in the moment with a positive attitude and find joyful moments that you might have otherwise missed. If you spend every minute Instagramming and Tweeting about the live concert, you are most likely to miss what is actually happening right in front of you. The key to happiness is making your dreams come true. Follow your vision without wavering. It very well may not be an easy road, but make your dreams happen. Aspiration is the greatest ally anyone can have on their rise to success. It gives you a reason to move forward despite trials and tribulations. Commitment is the breathtaking moment of making a compelling decision. Once commitment is made, indecision is eliminated. However, a commitment is not made lightly. It is about making a decision so strong that there is no going back. The decisive act of making a commitment to reach a goal propels us forward on our path. At each step along the way, our commitment inspires us to keep moving forward and overcome obstacles. Some people are scared of planning and setting future goals because they believe the disappointment of not meeting those goals has a higher chance than succeeding. Do not be this person. Allowing fear to stand in the way of your progress is silly. Overcome your fears so that you can move forward. Do not turn waiting into a habit. Stop waiting, go live your dreams right now because life is happening right now. Do not keep waiting for later, because later becomes never. Stop being so comfortable. Always be ready for change because life is unpredictable and you never know what might be coming next. Know that most things in your life are temporary. The greatest moments will not last forever, so take it in and enjoy it when you can. Also, the pains and hardships are not lasting, so know that you will overcome them. No matter how bad you fail. No matter how many times you screw up and think about quitting. Tell yourself to keep going. Demand persistence from yourself. Do not quit, because a month from now you will be much closer to your goal than you are now. Make every day count. You may be young, but that does not mean you have to be scared. Stop swallowing your words. Do not focus on other people's opinions. Do not live passive, do not over apologize when you have done nothing wrong, and do not regret being too nice. Be conscious of who you are allowing into your life. Avoid making unworthy people a priority in your life. Stop waiting for the next day. Live now, do what you want now. Take risks. This life is yours and it can only be what you make it. Researchers have given compelling evidence that strong relationships contribute to a long, healthy, and happy life. Do not just listen to people to be able to summarize what they are saying just to be able to reply. Listen to people to understand; understand the way they think and what it is they are really trying to communicate. Healthy relationships will only help you; they are a vital component of your health and wellbeing. Networking is the process of making connections. By establishing relationships and nurturing them you grow your human capital. Most likely, you are already networking without even being aware of it. By joining groups, playing sports, and getting to know new people, you are networking. In terms of job searching, networking is an effective, critical aspect. Networking opportunities are available both on and off campus. The key to successful networking is being able to tap into your sources and get job leads, recommendations, or advice from those with useful experience that you might not have. No one likes a greedy ass, so plan on giving back in some way as well.

Regardless of how old you are, where you live, or what your career goals are, everybody's ultimate goal in life is to be happy and successful. If you ask twenty successful people what the key to success is, you are likely to get a mixture of different answers with some notable similarities. As an entrepreneur, the key to business success is winning and building clientele. The key to winning and keeping customers is relationships. As a business woman we are told that spending time building your personal brand, growing your social media network, improving productivity, identifying and enhancing strengths, engaging employees, among other things, will make us successful. No matter what you do for a living or aspire to become, building real relationships with real people in the real world will have a palpable impact on how things turn out for you and your business. Why are relationships the key to business success? Most professionals say your most important asset is your network—not your virtual network or Instagram followers. One relationship in the real world is worth way more than 250k followers on Instagram or twitter. On the other hand, in today's world those 250k followers can be extremely beneficial towards having an audience to market to, but if your internet "fame" is not being capitalized on then it is of no material benefit. Sales transactions are between two real human beings, therefore, you will need to establish a real relationship if you are looking to make sales. Buyer behavior is mostly subjective and relationships are a key factor—the best product does not necessarily always win. You remember that golden rule you were taught in elementary school? "Do onto others as you would want them to do onto you." If you never knew that was known as the golden rule, you are not alone. Until one of my teammates referred to that saying as the golden rule I had forgotten all about it. As a salesperson or professional serve your clients as you would have them serve you. Meet their needs as you would want yours met. Give them prices you would expect to pay, exceed their expectations in a way that you would want your expectations to be exceeded. When you follow the golden rule, you open the door to success. As I said before, you cannot have success if you do not know what it means for you. Everyone views success differently and using someone else's standard for success does not necessarily equate success for you. Go through a thorough process of applying reason and critical thinking to determine validity. Your process will include you finding a supported conclusion, not the justification of a preconceived conclusion. In your own individual way, apply critical thinking to different aspects of your life. Do not simply debunk ideas you do not agree with. Being somewhat of a skeptic is essential and meaningful towards achieving success. There are tons of frauds out there and you should not believe everything you hear or see. Set clear and realistic goals that you will be able to realize when you have achieved them. Create quantifiable benchmarks that can give you a sense of satisfaction and completion, in return making you feel successful and confident. For instance, say right now you want to write a book, give yourself a realistic goal of completing a certain amount of pages within the next month. Albert Einstein once said that imagination is more important than knowledge. You have to actually imagine becoming successful. What does success look like in your life? Close your eyes right now and envision success. What do you want your legacy to be? How would you like to be remembered by others? How do you want to make your community a better place? What are your subjects of interest? The more vividly and accurately you imagine your success, the easier it will be for the rest of yourself to follow. Dedicate a few minutes each day to imagining your success. When you wake up and you are brushing your teeth imagine this: Imagine you are a character in a book about success. What is the first chapter? What are you doing in the book? Savor this feeling of your success and use it as motivation and inspiration to light your fire. Cultivate a healthy motivation when envisioning your success. Successful people all believe in themselves and their missions. At the same time, you do not want to alienate other people by having extreme narcissism. Less narcissistic people are respected more by co-workers, and happy co-workers make a more successful team. Furthermore, respect will make you successful. Keep your plans on the low, share them with those closest to you that you know have your best interest in mind. Understand that others want to be just as successful as you do and your goal should not be to trample over them to get what you want or to overshadow their own ambitions and goals. Be mindful of self and others while focusing on what is meaningful and important in your life. Inner happiness and fulfillment come when your mind, body, and emotions are nurtured by the choices you make. When we are in balance we make time for the things that are important to us. Staying in balance is an ongoing process about choices. We are constantly making choices about what we do, feel, think, or say. When questions arise about how we spend our time, we make choices depending on what is important in the moment. We may choose to give up time with friends to finish a project for class. Many of the choices we make every day like, work, school, sports, hobbies, friends, and family are about balance. Balance is not about rigidly devoting equal time to everything that matters to us, and it is not about totally immersing ourselves in one area of our lives. With improvement and balance comes success. Balance is about considering everything that is meaningful and important to us. When we find the right balance, we are happy, healthy, productive, and fulfilled.

Success means loving yourself, loving what you do, and loving how you do it. Confidence helps.

Chapter 4- Success in High School

Even though student debt is reaching heights of trillions of dollars, there is data that suggests going to college for four years is still worth it. News articles tell us that there is a pay gap between college graduates and people who have not earned a degree. There are not more college graduates than the economy needs and the trend in college graduates earning more money than non-graduates is expected to continue to grow. Although, the cost of college is the biggest discussion, we are told the big economic returns go to people with college diplomas. Thousands of students all over the world dream of being admitted to an Ivy League or an elite institution. Realize that the odds of getting into any of the country's most selective and elite colleges are quite remote. High grades and test scores do not guarantee admissions. Accomplishing acceptance to an Ivy school has become more and more difficult due to the rapidly growing applicant pool. Be realistic and you can most definitely increase your chances of getting into college and even an Ivy League college by taking notes on my following tips.

Challenge yourself; seek out rigorous and demanding opportunities at your high school, especially academic ones. If your school offers advanced courses, especially those with college credit, Ivy League schools will expect that you have taken them. It is helpful for you to take difficult classes and work hard in subjects you expect to continue with in college. You will impress colleges as well as gain an advantage above other students. During your high school career aim to be a well-rounded achiever. You should have a consistent history of high scholastic achievement and you will need to establish a high grade point average (GPA). Having a GPA in the top 10% of your class is essential. Being ranked among the top few students will certainly increase your odds of getting into an elite university. Get involved in extracurricular activities. Ivy Leagues want to see a well-rounded applicant who did not seclude themselves for four years in order to get good grades. Join a club, get involved in the theater department or a sports team. Volunteer your time and think on a national or international scale—you never have to limit yourself to opportunities only in your home town. Lead in the areas that you excel in. Look for opportunities where you can take on additional responsibility and recognition as a leader. This can range from being captain on your sports team to being president of your class. Whatever it is, take your job as a leader seriously. The lessons you learn in a leadership position can be experiences that separate you from the other applicants and give you skillsets to discuss in your essay or during your interview. Have excellent standardized test scores. This is critical because it is the one area where you are on equal footing with everyone else applying. Avoid taking the tests more than three times because the admission panel will notice this. Your repeated attempts to get a high score may come off as too obsessed with scores. So, be prepared before you take the test; take classes, practice tests, or get a few books. Speed and accuracy on these tests is a unique skill which needs to be learned, therefore, start preparing early and keep at it until you can solve the problems without much thinking. Ask teachers who know you well and have a favorable opinion of you to write a great recommendation on your behalf. Some will appreciate if you can make their job easier by providing them with a few notes for starting points on what to say about you. When applying to Ivies make sure to put in time and extensive research. Each Ivy offers their own experience. Find out if the academic opportunities the school offers, location, students, climate, professors, social life, dormitories, and food services are things you would enjoy for the next four years of your life. Research financial aid opportunities; although Ivy schools are notoriously expensive there are plenty opportunities for financial aid on a need basis. None of the Ivies give academic merit scholarships, they only give out money based on your financial need. After an all-encompassing research, plan a visit to the schools. Talk with professors and current students to get a sense of what your life there would be like. Try to see if you can spend a weekend there and get a feel for the social life. Begin your application process as early as possible so that you have ample time to revise anything. Ignore peoples advice on early admissions because applying early and being one of the first applications an admission officer sees is advantageous as opposed to the six hundred applications an admission office sees during the regular admissions period. Ask for advice, from anyone familiar with prestigious universities, on what to write about and how to best present them to school. The essay is very important and helps the admission officer get a feel for you and what you have to offer. Present your accomplishments and good qualities in a creative, self-aware manner. Make your essay memorable and be willing to take a risk in a tasteful manner that highlights your positive traits without coming across as a narcissist. Take time to think about what you want to present in your essay, do not try to write what you think the admissions people want to hear. Relax and write what you truly want to say. However, an amazing essay cannot save a bad application so your application needs to be strong academically. Admissions want to see a strong academic record, a winning essay, meaningful extracurricular activities, and good letters of recommendation. Interviews can be with the admissions office or alumni and can range from relatively nonchalant to interrogative. Be prepared, dress respectfully, and above all be you- in the mature version. Use your guidance counselor to do mock interviews, practice answering interview questions, and bounce ideas off of.

Then, sit back and wait for the results—what is meant to be will be.

Now what do you do after you have either been accepted or rejected? If you have been accepted go turn up! But, do not allow your grades to significantly slip and please do not get arrested. If you have been wait-listed your chances of being accepted are slim and it might be time to move onto your next choice. Students who fall within the statistical averages of the Ivy League but still do not gain acceptance, you did not get denied because of something you did wrong or because of something you were missing. Instead, there was someone else who helped fill an institutional priority or who has done something so unique that they were almost unrivaled. There are so many bright, capable, intellectually curious students who will not be Ivy bound, but will enrich the institution of his or her choice. If you are determined to graduate from an Ivy there is still the option of transferring into an Ivy. If you do outstanding work at a second tier school you can try transferring after a year or two. You might be able to skip repetitive introductory courses but you will most likely have to take four years of courses. Remember, your degree is only from the school where you finished and not where you began. There is also the option of graduate school programs from an Ivy League school. By doing exceptional work at an undergraduate program and performing very well on the appropriate admission exam (GRE, MCAT, LSAT) you can apply to an Ivy League graduate program. An elite graduate school can do a lot more to increase your income in a highly-paid profession than a prestigious undergraduate program would.

For those of you contemplating staying close to home rather than going away to college I am going to outline the benefits and drawbacks of each. I know how hard it can be to leave the comforts of our homes, but it is important that your decision is based on academic options, extracurricular activities, scholarships offers, and campus life. Room and board are expensive and being able to stay at home with your parents would definitely eliminate those costs, making tuition more affordable. Admissions and institutional funding can tremendously help with students who display a real financial aid. If funds for housing or tuition are a real concern then it may be best to stay close to home, but if other factors outweigh the costs then attending that more expensive school far away might be the better choice. A lot of parents are not comfortable with the thought of their child leaving home but your parents as well as you need to keep in mind that the closer school may not be the best choice for your success. That moment when your parents are driving away from your college marks a new chapter in your life. Many students go away to college only to find that the transition is more pressure than they are ready to handle. Living with a roommate you barely know, new social pressures, homesickness, and the challenge of college courses can induce high levels of stress. Just know that as time goes on you learn how to maneuver you campus climate and you will start to learn ways to deal with campus problems; this will increase your maturity and life skills. On the other hand, plenty new freshmen embrace the new adventures of going away to school. The opportunity to direct your own schedule and make decisions for yourself will create a clear distinction between high school and college. Living away from home during your time in college is a learning experience. Going away to college teaches you how to live independently. With no parents immediately around college students must learn to fend for themselves, balance their budgets, and deal with problems on their own. Learning to navigate life in a new place gives students memories and experiences that they will have for the rest of their lives and the chance to see what life is like somewhere besides home. Another benefit of going away to college is that it gives you the chance to have totally new experiences and relationships you would never have had if you remained at home. Living with a roommate can lead to developing a new life-long best friend. You will have the opportunity to get to know people who come from different backgrounds than you. Going away will teach you how to live with and tolerate others. Residence hall life gives you the chance to meet people who have different morals, values, political views or religious vies. Although students living at home can still join groups and organizations, being in the midst of campus activities gives you a stronger, immediate connection to the university and its community. Students who commute or live at home do not often have time to attend social functions, participate in campus groups or immerse themselves daily in campus life. Students who live on campus are within walking distance to everything that happens on campus. You can spend a year or two saving money then move to a dorm or apartment near campus.

If you are smart enough to get into an Ivy, then you would be smart enough to research which Ivy is best for you. Prior to 1954 there was no official athletic conference known as the Ivy League. The member schools that later became known as the Ivy League always had close connections prior to the coining. Since its inception, the Ivy League membership has remained static, a contrast to the seismic shifts faced by other conferences across the nation. While each of the members share many common characteristics such as: academic prestige, in-depth history, and enormous price-tags, each still have some unique features that differentiate them. The colleges are in constant competition with each other and each college insists that they are the best, thus, creating strong bonds within and between the different schools.

Harvard is widely known for being great at damn near everything. When it comes to the Ivy League, Harvard is the granddad of them all. The college is located in Cambridge, Massachusetts, near Boston, the area of intellectual enlightenment occupied with recent graduates. Regardless, of which school tops any given ranking in any given year, no college can exceed the prestige and reputation of Harvard. Harvard was the first higher learning institution in the United States and had the largest endowment in the world. The red bricked halls carry a feeling of history and grandeur. This feeling is heightened from the university being filled with more tourists than students. Athletically they are known as the "crimson red." Yale is located in New Haven, Connecticut, a decent city with a tarnished reputation for violence. More so than the other Ivies, Yale feels as if it belongs in old England. Yale's buildings were modeled-off traditional English universities, which give the school an old English feel. Also, Yale has a strong emphasis on the traditional residential college system as developed by schools like Oxford and Cambridge. Yale students are assigned to one of the twelve residential colleges, where they live during their time at Yale. Yale is known to be great at humanities and social sciences. Their mascot is the bulldog. Of the eight Ivies, Princeton is the ivy-est of them all. Princeton is located in the "farmlands" of Princeton, New Jersey. Princeton embodies the traditional feel of what it means to be in the Ivy League. Ancient-looking buildings covered in ivy make the university the stereotypical Ivy League school. Princeton has unique eating clubs and independent coed organization that take the role of both dining hall and fraternity. These eating clubs are housed in historic mansions, further adding to the Ivy League stereotype. Their mascot is a tiger. The most distinguishing thing about Columbia is its location. Columbia is located in Morningside Heights of upper Manhattan, where there is plenty to do in New York City. While the University is rather enclosed, with two full blocks making up the center of the campus, it is hard to forget that the school is only a few-minute taxi ride away from the heart of New York City's financial district. With a large student body of about 7,000 undergraduates and a heavy concentration of approximately 15,000 graduate students, Columbia is the definition of an urban school. There athletic nickname is the lions. Dartmouth is located in suburban Hanover, New Hampshire. Dartmouth has the smallest undergraduate student body of the Ivies with approximately 4,000 undergraduate students. Dartmouth is known as the unique Ivy because of all the Ivies Dartmouth seems to be the most unlike its peers. Dartmouth is known for its focus on undergraduate education; it insists on being called

Dartmouth College, instead of university, because the school does not fit the traditional definition of a university. The location of Dartmouth, in the tiny neighborhood of Hanover, contrast to the neighborhoods of Ivies residing in more urban areas. Dartmouth has a unique quarter schedule system known as the D-plan, where rising juniors are required to attend school during the summer and take off a quarter during the traditional academic year. This allows Dartmouth students to avoid the heavy competition for summer internships and other educational opportunities. We also have the most unique, unofficial mascot, Keggy the Keg. Brown has a liberal arts research university feel. Located in Providence, Rhode Island it has a similar feel like Boston, but more subdued. Brown has a more relaxed and laidback feel compared to the other ivies. It is quitter and escapes the hustle and bustle of the other urban schools. Brown has an open curriculum in which Brown undergraduates have virtually no required courses. Unlike most liberal arts schools which require students to take multiple interdisciplinary classes, Brown leaves the choice up to the students; ensuring that they are never forced to take a class they do not want. Brown has one of the more well-fitting nicknames, as the brown bears. Cornell is located in Ithaca, Upstate New York. The school has the largest amount of undergraduate students with approximately 14,000 undergrads. Cornell has the interesting description of being both a private and public land-grant university. Due to this, some schools within Cornell receive state funding and are therefore, somewhat considered public. While this interesting split makes little difference today, of all the Ivies Cornell feels the closet to a traditional public university with a relatively large student body in a picturesque college-town and without sacrificing the Ivy League academic prestige. Cornell's athletic nickname is the big red. The University of Pennsylvania is located in Philadelphia, Pennsylvania. While the University of Pennsylvania was not the first of the ivies to be established, it is rich with history and was the first American university to reach many important milestones. Benjamin Franklin founded the university in 1740 as the first secular college in America. It opened the nation's first medical school in 1765. Also, the university houses the nation's first business school and first student union. Athletically they are known as the Quakers.

The transition from elementary to middle school to high school can be difficult. It is not uncommon for new high school students to struggle academically their first year. My first year of high school I went to public school. Luckily, my grades never suffered, but the atmosphere in a public school differs vastly from the catholic, private school I transferred to my sophomore year. Colleges recognize that performance during the first year of high school is not the best indicator of a student's ability, dedication, or intelligence. If you have performed poorly during your first year of high school there is still hope. If you really want to attend a top public college or university just make sure your academic performance improves during your sophomore, junior, and senior years. If you struggle academically your freshman year in high school and fail to show a marked improvement in your performance in subsequent years, you may find yourself attending a two-year community college in order to prove to an admissions board that you can handle the demands of a four-year college or university. However, getting good grades alone is not enough to get you into a public ivy. Students considering getting into a public ivy might want to consider my following tips.

Admissions officers know which high schools are tough and which ones are not. Top public ivy admission officers will take into consideration the difficulty level of your high school's curriculum when making their decision. Consequently, if your grades are not excellent but you are attending a high school that offers a very challenging curriculum, you still have a great chance at being admitted. College admission officers are interested in determining whether or not an applicant has the skills, dedication, and knowledge to handle the rigors and fast pace of college. Students who enroll in difficult courses in high school, like advanced placement classes and honors courses demonstrate to colleges that they have what it takes to succeed in college. Even if you have a high grade point average you might not get into a top college if you have only been taking the easiest classes your high school offers. Earning a "B+" in advanced placement chemistry is going to be more impressive than getting an "A+" in home economics. If you do not do well in high school but believe you have the smarts. Attending a junior or community college after high school can prove to public ivies that you have what it takes. Still be prepared to work hard. Junior and community colleges are more demanding than high schools. It is far easier to do well in high school and go directly into the four-year college of your choice. Colleges are looking for students that have demonstrated over several years that they are prepared for college. Besides the well-known "requirements" or pre-requisites for applying to an Ivy League school like good grades, near perfect standardized test scores, strong extracurricular activity, and leadership roles, there are other qualities that set the admitted students apart from the masses of smart, talented, enthusiastic applicants that Ivies receive every year. A desire for knowledge is indispensable. As a student, attending college equates to learning more. While some individuals seek college with the sole purpose of finding a post-graduation job, Ivy League material students should enjoy learning and hope to gain an enriching experience at an Ivy League college. The student's own enjoyment of learning should be cultivated and nurtured through the various classes the student chooses, and his or her interactions with teachers and mentors. Signs of taking initiative are imperative. Students at Ivy League schools do not just spend their time on academics. We take the initiative to get involved in our community. Taking initiative can happen in different ways, from chasing an idea and creating a startup, to opening a club on campus, to asking an upperclassmen or advisor for advice on how to maximize the resources available. Know what your passions are and cultivate a focus. Apart from the desire to learn, Ivy League students tend to have an area of focus, a topic that interests them the most that influences not only what classes they take, what organizations they join, but also shapes their future aspirations. While these passions are in a flux, by having a concentration, students are able to work towards specific goals and act according to plan. This contributes to the diversity at Ivies and also means that students connect with various individuals who have different interests. Be you, be your own individual... be unique. During the application process there will be thousands of applicants who have good grades, good test scores, and strong leadership skills. What really sets you apart is your uniqueness, your philosophy behind why you do things the way you do. It is important that you show the admissions officers that you have a story. Your narrative should tie together the various activities you participate in and the classes that you work on and enjoy the most. In addition, every individual comes from a different background and has lived through distinctive experiences. Your story should explain how you have digested the experiences you have had and how they have contributed to your accomplishments. By crafting an application this way, you can set yourself apart from the rest of the applicant pool—who may have the same grades, but not the same story. Showcase your ability to overcome obstacles. Whether creating a startup, charity, club on campus or taking an exasperating class or extracurricular, students will always face obstacles. A common characteristic of Ivy League students is the ability to identify these difficulties and overcome them. By understanding your goals, your obstacles, and what you must do to overcome them, you will be better equipped to tackle any problems that come your way. It is important that when a hurdle does arise, you do not give up or get frustrated, instead dismantle the problem and resolve it piece by piece.

If you dream of attending a highly selective college with state of the art facilities, but dread the thought of dishing out a small fortune in tuition, you still have options. Among the nation's most competitive schools are several public universities, often referred to as the "Public Ivies." Public Ivies are considered to be capable of successfully competing with the Ivy League schools in academic rigor. If you qualify for state residency at any of these institutions, you could pay up to $25,000 less in tuition each year than at the private Ivy League colleges. Another difference between public ivies and private ivies is the number of students. Some of the Public Ivies are: University of California at Berkeley, University of Wisconsin, University of Michigan, Pennsylvania State University at University Park, Georgia Institute of Technology, University of Florida, University of North Carolina, University of Virginia, University of Washington, State University of New York at Binghamton, College of William and Mary, and University of California at Los Angeles. Even the largest Ivy, Cornell with about 14,000 undergraduates enrolled, is only one-third the size of the University of Florida. So if you seek a high level of instruction and a big college experience these colleges are a good choice. Public ivies are consistently ranked among the top schools in the United States and can be found numerous articles among the top ranked graduate schools in business, education, engineering, law, and medicine. One sharp distinction between the Ivy League and some public ivies is their participation in intercollegiate athletics. One of the Ivy League's distinguishing characteristics is its prohibition on the awarding of athletic scholarship. As an

Ivy League athlete you may only receive the same financial aid to which you would be entitled even if you did not play a sport. In contrast, many of the public ivies participate in major athletic conferences such as the Big 12, Big Ten, ACC, Pac-12, or SEC, and award athletic scholarships. These schools sometimes rely on profits, if any, from large scale football and men's basketball programs to support the athletic department as a whole. Other elite schools exist as well. Depending on whom you talk to some will say the most difficult colleges to get into are neither Ivy League schools nor Public Ivies. A diverse range of colleges, including the Massachusetts Institute of Technology (MIT), the Julliard School, and the United States Military Academy, are known to be extremely selective. They represent a small sample of the other elite schools that are extremely competitive, offer outstanding academic programs, and attract the best and the brightest students and faculty. Many of these elite colleges, such as Stanford, Notre Dame, Duke, and Vanderbilt, are well known. Typically, not always, these colleges are similar in atmosphere to the Ivy League schools. They often have relatively small enrollments, diverse yet competitive student bodies, and rigorous course loads. They can also charge a small fortune, with many like Bowdoin College, George Washington University, and Wesleyan University costing even more than the Ivy League schools. With high tuition, large endowments, and countless federal grants, the elite colleges can often afford to hire the best professors and purchase the latest equipment and facilities. Add small class sizes and meaningful student to faculty interactions to the ingredients, and you have a recipe for academic success. The elite colleges attract the top-notch faculty, students, and staff. Those who have excelled in their fields naturally want to surround themselves with other accomplished individuals. Still, the elite colleges do an admirable job of creating extremely diverse student bodies.One of the most considerable differences between Ivy League schools and other competitive liberal arts schools is their reputation. Even the most prestigious private and state universities do not have the reputation that Ivy League schools carry. The title, "Ivy League" alone separates them from the pack. There are benefits associated with having an Ivy League education, such as high employment rates, high paying jobs and favoritism with employers. I have even heard that job recruiters often target Ivy League graduates because they view them as sure bets in the workplace. Also, take into consideration the location of the Ivy schools. All eight Ivies are located on the East Coast. If you prefer to live in a certain part of the country or want to stay close to home, the location of Ivy League schools might be a major consideration. Because all Ivy League schools are private, the tuition costs are higher for students compared to their in-state public tuition alternative. However, Ivy League schools have the reputation for being generous with financial aid due to their large endowments. A lot of students come from the top quartile of the income spectrum, which makes Ivies an elite institution not just in academic quality but also in derivation. It is harder than you think and it takes long range planning to get into the Ivy League. Although, there are many quality colleges and universities in the United States, every year a disproportionate number of high school seniors try to get into a very small group of admitted Ivy-Leaguers. As a student or parent there are several essential tools for success at the top: a strong strategic admissions plan, an outstanding student profile, and good advice along the way. In your early years, get involved with your school's guidance program, look for signs of special talents, and increase involvement with teachers and administrators. Once, your grade point average (GPA) and class rank start to accumulate continue excelling. Excel in academics and extracurricular activities. Do not waste your summers. Look for shadow internship experiences or any chances where you can spend time during your summers being productive. As you get older continue to develop extracurricular interests, sharpen your writing skills and vocabulary, and pursue your academic strengths. Take preparation SATs and start looking at college candidates.

Or, maybe you are thinking about taking a gap year, perhaps taking a year or two off from college. Making smart decisions requires time and research, but not necessarily time away from college. The passing of time by itself will not make the decision any easier to reach. On the other hand, taking away the pressure for an immediate decision is wise. If this is the decision you are going to make put your time and energy to the best use. Allow yourself a semester to take several explorations, conduct informative interviews, and gather the information you need to reach a satisfying decision.

Chapter 5- Success in College

The Ivy League is made up of eight private institutions: Dartmouth College, Princeton University, Harvard University, Cornell University, Brown University, Yale University, Columbia University, and the University of Pennsylvania (UPenn).These institutions are some of the nation's oldest schools that are known for academic excellence, social elitism, and selectivity in admissions. It was football that established the Ivy League as an early athletic conference that evolved into a collection of the country's most selective institutions. The Ivy League schools are often ranked among the best universities worldwide. These schools are highly selective and have low acceptance rates in comparison to the thousands of applicants the respective admissions offices receive. The students being admitted are the needle in the haystack of college-bound applicants. Of course, you want to know more about whom these people are right? Some may complain and moan that there is leniency for athletes and legacies, but these schools would not take an athlete who will be successful on the field, but has very limited ability to succeed in the classroom. Nor, would these schools take a son or daughter of an alum that has no academic success or ability to thrive at an Ivy League institution. These days most people recognize the Ivy League schools as representing the pinnacle of academic superiority. But it is not just high-achieving students who are attracted to these colleges. The professors at Ivy League schools come from the upper echelon of their fields as well. Add to their stellar reputation, a list of alumni who have become leaders in the worlds of business, politics, and the fine arts, and the result is an unequaled level of selectivity. The great thing about higher education in the United States is that if you dream big, work hard, and have a personality that shines through, you may just be the right fit for one of these elite schools. Elite colleges have far more applicants than slots, so they can pretty much make their campuses look any way they want. For the most part, they understand the importance of a diverse student body. My classmates come from upper, middle, and lower economic classes and from various countries, states, cultures, races, and nationalities. As Ivy leaguers we generally have three things in common: superior academic records, a drive to be the absolute best, and the confidence that big things are headed our way. Becoming a college student is not about good grades it is about your mindset. You get what you put in. Having a positive mindset and applying that mindset will help you become a successful student despite your grades. Confidence is important in every aspect of life. Being confident as a student dictates your success in a class. Having a spirit of conquering anything that comes your way and having a strong confidence of succeeding is vital to your college success. If you want to go to college and have academic achievements, advance your life management, and improve your social relations then these tips will assist you in your pursuit of success. Academic achievements involve good grades, improved educational skills, career-oriented activities, and notable academic milestones. Academic achievement is equally as important as academic engagement; high grades are great, but engaging in the material you are being taught even if it is a challenging course has real rewards like self-discovery and true understanding. Social relations incorporate you making new friends, maintaining those friendships, experiencing romance, and extracurricular activities. Life management includes your well-being, work ethic, balance in your life, and overall happiness and satisfaction with college. For many students, the biggest difference between college and high school is the amount of personal responsibility you have. There is no one there to tell you what to do. Getting to class, doing the homework, and turning assignments in on time are all tasks you have to complete without a parent or teacher overseeing your decisions. First, make sure you actually show up to class. Then, do not just show up to class, but get involved. Large lecture halls can be very intimidating. When you are actively engaged in the class asking questions or presenting your opinions, rather than just going through the motions, you will get a better grasp on the material and increase your chances of getting better grades on your following exams. I can recommend sitting at the front of the room or close to the professor in order for you to feel more present, but if you do not feel comfortable in the front you can still fully participate elsewhere in the classroom. When it comes to class it is important to take notes. I do not know how you can come to class with no pen, paper, or computer. To me it is a waste of your time and you would be better off spending your time sleeping. You might think you do not need to take notes because you can just listen and learn, but chances are you will not remember everything. Maybe you are lucky enough and your professor posts their notes online so you plan to just get the notes when you want. Chances are you will not understand everything or you end up putting off printing the notes until it is actually test-taking time. However, taking notes is the key essential to retaining the information from lectures. Adjust your attention span. I know how used to getting our content in short, entertaining clips we are with our generation of 2 minute how to YouTube videos, abbreviated text messages, and 140 character tweets. But, professors like to use 60 or more minute lectures to give us the information needed to pass their course. Retrain your attention span to process long units of content rather than zoning in and out of things. Quit the procrastination sooner than later. Some college students do well under pressure, but setting time to complete tasks will give you more ease to focus on different tasks and significantly ease your stress level; giving you more time for sleeping or partying—and what college student does not love to sleep or party? Make sure that in the chaos of classes and your other college activities that you find time to eat healthy, exercise, and get enough rest. Organize your time; time-management is a key tool to capitalize on during your time in college. Organize your goals by the level of importance they have. Take time for yourself to do whatever you want to do. Learn to balance work, play, and the hundred other things in between. Eat lean meat or protein, fruits and vegetables, and whole grains. Stay away from the late night calls for pizza and Chinese, the excess beer (beer belly), and the saturated fats and candies. Not only will you feel better, but you will be in a better position to avoid the infamous freshman fifteen. Exercise helps us burn fat, build muscle, lower cholesterol, ease stress, and sleep better. If you are not on a sports team or intramural team try to get at least 30 minutes of exercise and stay away from the lazy mentality—take the stairs instead of the elevator or wake up a little early and walk to class instead of taking the shuttle. One of the best ways to maximize academic performance on tests is getting a good night's sleep. Students who pull all-nighters or routinely stay up all night on weekends develop sleep disorders and perform worse in college than students who get regular, comfortable, lasting sleep—why stress your body so much at such a young age? Visit your campus health center and take advantage of the free amenities the center offers: free vaccines, condoms, and counseling among other things. Be aware of your limit and know when things are out of your control. Sometimes you will have to withdraw from courses; if it is better for you to withdraw from a certain course than fail, do it. If you need a tutor, get one. Know your limit and if you have reached it do not be afraid to ask for assistance. Get involved during your time in college. Make sure to make time to socialize and establish new friendships. If you are at a big school, move past your intimidation and find people you can hang with and learn from. Often, people will say it was the friendships and people around them that made their college years so memorable. College students who are involved in any extracurricular activities are more likely to be better students. Join clubs, traditions, or events where you have the opportunity to meet people that share a similar interest with you. If you already have an established immediate social circle, take the time to meet people outside of that—do you not get annoyed and bored with seeing your same teammates, sorority sisters, fraternity brothers every day? If you think you might enjoy the party life, go out! Try the party scene and put a smile on your face and get in the mood for meeting new people. Be a gracious party-goer, because nobody like a Debby downer and only a rare few (not the type of people you want to be around) enjoy a sloppy drunk. When someone host a party or kickback in their room, do not make a mess—it is just rude. Be careful about drugs and never do anything you are not comfortable doing. Remember that more often than not, you do not know what is in a particular drug. If you decide to have sex, always make it consensual and safe. People will brag about sex and talk about it constantly, but never feel that you are pressured into having sex. Most of them talking about it are not even getting any. If you are sexually active, whether you are a guy or a girl, always keep a condom on you or in your dorm. Understand that alcohol will mess with your judgment or decision making skills. Alcohol will decrease your inhibitions and make it easier for you to justify having sex with someone you might not have if you were sober. Use your school's safety officers or cab services to escort you home or to your dorm if you feel unsafe. If you have been a victim of any type of crime do not be afraid to notify your campus security or local police. Knowing and using your on-campus resources are a valuable source to use to secure your safety. Colleges also offer extensive resources to help you succeed in your academics, extracurricular activities, and career growth. By the end of your freshman year you should aim to be familiar with the best study spot location that suites your needs, your dean or academic advisor's office, the academic support center, and the career services center. Find out what sources are available and what sources you can utilize for your benefit. Counselors, writing workshops, tutors, career advisors, and reference librarians are all willing to help and want to provide assistance so make the best use of them. There are too many pressures these days for students to declare a major very early in their first year. Unless you are 1000000... percent sure, without any doubt, do not declare and set your mind to one major early on in your college career. A better idea is to take two classes in the field you think you want to major in while taking other classes in other fields you might have an interest in— or simply to try something new. Amidst all the distribution courses, general education requirements, prerequisites, and major or minor requirements, it is easy to forget what your intellectual interests were in the first place. Each semester try to takes at least one course in something you are good at or intrigued by. The joy of learning something you enjoy will go a long way in your college experience and you will most likely gain some general education or distribution credit too. Your major choice or occupation decision are not irreversible. As you grow and learn more about yourself do not be afraid of change in other areas of your life. There are probably several careers that match your interests, abilities, and personality. Many of college graduates obtain employment in areas unrelated to their college major. Unfortunately, there is no perfect test to tell you what career path to follow. Taking different career test can provide some helpful information for career planning, but it will not provide all of the answers. You are the only expert on yourself. Career counselors can assist you in the planning process, but only you can determine the best choice for you. Counselors and the career center can help you clarify your interests, skills, personality, or decision-making patterns. Being undecided is normal. Being undecided is not a sign of immaturity or adolescent. Well-defined career interests have more to do with experience than maturity level. Interest do not firmly establish until you are out of college. Most college students do not have a clear idea of what they want to major in or do for the rest of their lives. This is normal. With proper research and support, you can make decisions that are right for you. There are different combining elements of your interest that determine career satisfaction and various careers. For example, if you like helping people in an artistic way, you may find enjoyment in being an art teacher or acting coach. Most majors prepare you for a variety of careers. When you combine the skills you will learn in your major with other skills you will gain from internships, work experience, socializing, and other activities, you will create the ability to move in an assortment of directions. Most people have multiple careers and jobs during their work lives. You only fail when you do not adapt. If you learn a major or career choice is not the best fit for you, change it. Collect enough information to make a calculated decision about your major or career choice. Realize that even after you make a decision, you will still be able to collect more information and evaluate further along in your journey. Pick a major that incorporates your skills and not just an interesting topic. Consider how to incorporate your natural aptitudes into what you will be learning about every class. Do not shy away from a liberal arts degree. You will be more than equip from the skills you develop in a liberal arts curriculum. Communication, analysis, flexibility, and human interaction are few of the skills you will develop and some of the most desired by employers. Researchers are trying to show that some college majors are less valuable than others. These researchers use statistics of high initial unemployment rates and low initial earnings to attempt to illustrate certain majors as being a waste of time and financial investment. There are big benefits to not believing everything the news tells you. Even though, the job market is difficult to predict it is important to look at the potential for employment. Look at the demand in your job market during your first year of college and what it is projected to look like at the time of your expected graduation. You will be much firmer grounded when you select a course of study that accurately interests you, and you find a way to apply it to a career or job. You do not necessarily have to pursue a certain specific major in order to prepare for professional schools like dentistry, law, business, or medicine. As long as you meet the certain academic courses, most professional and graduate schools do not require a specific major. Lately, we can see that liberal arts majors have had a greater success with acceptance to medical schools than biology majors. Some colleges offer advising programs for students who plan on attending medical school, law school, or graduate school. If you are planning to continue your education in professional or graduate programs you should know that you do not have to pick a major directly related to your future field. Do some research on your potential professors and the class syllabus. Ask yourself, is this someone I feel I can actually learn from? Does this class have a clear point? Am I really going to be engaged in this class? If you answer no to these questions do more class shopping. Students should pick classes and activities that will advance their knowledge and experience toward their career path. In addition, these classes and activities should be usable on a resume or during an interview. When you make that awesome sculpture in your art class, or get back that amazing thirty page research paper you might want to save it to show how your work exemplifies your creative ability and capability to write and think. Communicate with your professors and classmates. Communications with your professors will help them get to know you personally. Communicate with your classmates because you never know when you might need them— like that day you were "sick"(hung-over) and needed notes for the midterm. Listen to other students, but form your own opinions. Listen to other student's opinions on which classes are interesting, or which classes are "easy" because there is some degree of truth, but do not let them dissuade you from what you want to do. You are your own person and you need to form your own opinions. Connecting with your professor or teacher's assistant at office hours is a very underutilized resource. Professors are required to be in their office two to four hours a week to meet with students and provide help with the course. A common misconception about college faculty members is that they do not want to be bothered by students, but most professors encourage interaction outside the class. Trust me, your tests and papers will go better if you have had a chance to ask about things you are confused about. You might even receive some guidance from the professor about what you should be writing or what is going to be on the test. Demonstrating dedication and persistence to professors and teaching assistants will be helpful to you during time when you are struggling, stressing, or do not think you will be able to finish an assignment on time. Set time to study, then actually study. Study when it is best for you; when you have a clear mind, free from distractions, and take study breaks because let's be real that shit gets old. Some people like study groups, some prefer complete silence, and some like myself need television or music in the background. Find out what habits work best for you. Also, find out what kind of learner you are. Are you an auditory learner, who learns by hearing something, or a visual learner who learns by seeing something, or a kinesthetic learner who learns by actively touching or building something? Most of the work you will do for college is done outside the classroom. As soon as the semester starts find a study spot and block out the times of the week you are actually going to study and review material. Before the day of your exam construct a pre-test with study guide questions. At the actual exam write full answers that draw from the course materials. Make sure your writing would be clear to any capable reader. Always answer exactly the question asked. More points are lost on tests and papers by not answering the question asked, rather than giving the wrong answer. Even when you are stumped and have no clue what the answer is apply something from the course lectures, readings, or class discussion But, do not dump everything you know about the subject or simply ramble garbage. When you get your test back go over any comments your instructor has written and answer the question again in your head given the new information. Do not just throw it on the ground because that is just not beneficial to you or the environment. Budget your expenses. At this time in your life you are starting to take on adult responsibilities and it is time for you to learn how to manage your money. Take an inventory of the money you will have during any given month and budget out how much you will allow yourself to spend during that month. While many students still have their parents take care of their finances, make an effort to get your own credit card and pay some attention to your spending habits. Do you have an interest in studying abroad? Save money! Studying abroad cost money, you will want to eventually pay of those student loans, you will want spending money during college, and you will need it once you graduate. Are you ready for a long-term relationship with Sallie Mae? Do not delay thinking about the future until you have your diploma in your hands. If you do this you will most likely regret your lack of foresight and use of your school's resources during your time as an undergrad. To avoid getting stuck in a post-graduation rut or becoming unemployed make sure you are checking in with you goals every couple months and keep these questions in the back of your mind: When I graduate where will I be living? Where will I be working? Do I have the money to support myself for the next two years? You would be amazed by how helpful these internal conversations can be, rather than simply ignoring the reality of going into the post-graduation world. One of the best bridges between the classroom and corporate America is an internship. Internships and work experience are fundamental if you want to compete in today's tough economy. An internship does more than just look good on your resume. Interning gives you real world experience. If you intern at a company that relates to the industry you have studied you will get to see firsthand how the lessons you have been taught actually apply. A lot of times our visions of certain industries or companies are much different than reality. Doing an internship can benefit your decision to pursue a specific field and even help narrow down what position you would like to get. Interning in college or even before can help you determine what you want to do—saving you time and frustration early in your career. To get the most out of an internship, you need to put the most effort into it. Professionalism, enthusiasm, and willingness to perform whatever tasks are asked of you, are crucial. While you will be eager to show your capabilities and potential, remember that you are there to learn. You will impress your employers the most by listening, observing and completing the tasks you are given in a timely manner. This will build your trust between your employer and lead you to gaining more responsibility. Ask questions. If you have an actual interest in the job then you will want to get all your questions about the industry answered directly from those who know it best. Asking questions shows an eagerness and willingness to learn, which can go a long way with an employer. Do not wait until the last minute to start thinking about internships or applying for internships. By thinking about the process earlier you will increase your chances of landing the internship of your choice. Summer internships fill up fast because they receive a lot of applicants. Make sure you have an up to date resume and cover letter ready to go at all times. Interning on your semesters off is important for constructing your work experience, networking, and building your resume. Apply what you learn in college to your work environment. Learn hands on what you want to eventually do when you graduate. If you are unsure of where or how to start looking for internships, make a trip to the career services office. Career service advisors have all the information and resources your school has available. The career services may be able to show you how to access several different internship databases or get in contact with useful alumni in the industry you are looking at. If you have some companies and businesses in mind that you would like to intern for, research more about their internship programs. There might not be information online so do not by shy, give them a call. Personal referrals can ensure that your application will be read and considered.

Some of the good and bad things that happen in your uncanny four years: you see everyone you have ever hooked up with in a one-hour timespan. Your friends live three doors down from you You can always find free food.

Hangovers become tolerable. Taking shots is a normal occurrence. You do not have to plan anything ahead. You have to tolerate 20 other people's bathroom habits. The older guy you are crushing on will become a lawyer or doctor. You have seasonal breaks, You drink on Tuesdays, Wednesdays, Thursdays, Fridays, and Saturdays. You never have to wake up before 10a.m. Deadlines are adjustable. Getting ready to go out is not a chore. You do not wear heels to go out. You drink flavored vodka. Finding an outlet is a life or death situation. You make best friends at night, and then avoid eye contact with them the next day. You will own your walk of shame. You have no shame walking around in sweats. You have the right to say no to others' expectations of you and make your own career choices.

College is special time in your life and an experience unlike any other. You most likely gained new independence, you are in a new place, and your adult life is gradually staring you in the face. You have choices to make and need to figure out the best way to make them. Everyone does college differently, in their own style, but most students who succeed share certain qualities. Since college is a hefty investment of your time and money you should want to do what it takes to ensure that you will be a successful college student. In brief, make sure you do the following: develop a college plan, identify you goals and priorities, prepare academically during high school, prepare financially for college, manage your time, practice good money management, ask for advice, and see your academic advisor, maneuver around roadblocks, and most importantly enjoy and make the most of your college experience.

Chapter 6- What's Next?

Other than a degree, what will you gain from college?

A college education will expose you to a wide range of subject areas and will help you build and expand a well-rounded knowledge base. Your abstract thinking, critical thinking, decision making, problem solving, and communication skills will be refined. These skills will ascertain to be exceptionally useful in your personal and professional life. You will meet a lot of different types of people. Some of these people will become your friends for life—when you eat, sleep, and play together in your college bubble, relationships get deep fast. You will learn indispensable people skills that are central to your future success. You will learn how to analyze people, how to communicate with others, as well as how to build meaningful relationships. After college you will continuously build relationships with people you interact with and thanks to college you will be able to connect with people on a deeper level. College gives you exposure to multicultural activities and in today's globalized and diverse society, exposure to multicultural worlds is a must if you want to distinguish yourself. As a professional you never know where you may end up working and in our globalized economy who knows you could end up working in India, China or Spain. Each level of education you complete increases your chances of earning a higher salary. As you apply for various jobs your education will always come up at some point in the job application process. Applicants with a college education are more likely to be offered a job and keep it for an extended period of time, compared to someone with a high school diploma or General Education Development (GED) certificate. Every level of completed education will increase your chances of landing a good job. As students we have to handle rigorous workloads that give us the ability to work in high pressure situations. Not everything in the world goes according to plan, but learning how to adjust and adapt is crucial to the future of your success. The analytical and problem solving skills you learn from class allow you to approach different life scenarios conceptually. If you have not already thought about the importance of networks, do not fret because you will start your networking in college.

What if the Ivy League or a four-year college is just not in the cards for you? Then consider attending a community college where you can get an associate degree, or a certificate program, or technical training. The overall college experience, filled with personal growth and expanded horizons, will benefit your life. A college education is an investment that will pay you back for a lifetime if you follow my advice. Your career depends on you so give yourself the best chance to succeed

---

So you are determined or destined to play professionally? Division I and II schools provide billions of dollars in athletic scholarships annually to more than hundreds of thousands student-athletes. Division III schools do not offer athletically related financial aid. Only about two percent of high school students make up the student-athletes being awarded athletic scholarships to compete in college. Many athletic scholarships are granted per the academic year. Schools are allowed to provide multi-year scholarships, which would give you more assurance that your education will continue even if you suffer an injury, your coaches end up not liking you, or you have a coaching staff change. If you negotiate a full scholarship this will cover tuition and fees, room and board, and required course-related books. Usually, student-athletes receive athletic scholarships that only cover a portion of these costs. As a student-athlete you can receive other non-athletics financial aid such as Federal Pell Grants and the NCAA Division I Student-Athlete Opportunity Fund program. Once you accept your scholarship you will be asked to make a binding commitment to the school as your National Letter of Intent (NLI), which will be accompanied by an athletics scholarship. The odds of becoming a professional athlete are extremely small. Does that mean you cannot become one? Absolutely not, because you are the only person that controls your destiny—not statistics. But, taking calculated risks involves taking a look at the facts. You can look up the statistics, but I can save you the trouble by telling you the fact is majority of student-athletes will not become a high-paid, endorsed, professional athlete. Of the student-athletes participating in sports with professional leagues only very few will go on to becoming professional athletes. In reality, most student-athletes depend on academics to prepare them for their lives after college. The fame and fortune of being a professional athlete can be very attractive to an athlete in high school or college who is trying to figure out what to do with their life. What is better than taking something you know you are really good at and making lot of money with it? What a young athlete needs to be aware of are the facts. The number of high school athletes that actually go on to play college and professional sports is extremely competitive. No one wants to crush you dreams. If you think you have got what it takes, then, go pursue your dream. However, it is important to be realistic. Unlike plenty of my friends, establish a backup plan. If you are skilled enough or lucky enough to make the cut, keep in mind injuries do happen.

What defines "the real world?" What makes it real, and what makes the rest

unreal? What are the characterizations of "the real world?" How have we

socially constructed "the real world?" And is there any room for our

imaginations and dreams in "the real world?"

For most, the real world pertains to the actual experiences you will have

outside of your college life or home life. Prior to entering the real world some

may feel excited, overjoyed, and ready, while others may feel apprehensive,

shy and unprepared. If you have experienced life post-graduate or heard what

it is like from older friends you may have heard that the real life is mundane

and uninteresting or maybe you heard the complete opposite, that it is

amazing and freeing. Every person will have his or her own experience based

on his or her own interests and personality, but I will give you a briefing on

"the real world" and what to expect. Life is full of frightening transitions, but

do not fear the transition into the real world. Without you even knowing, you

were groomed for this moment for years. On college campuses, students are

often told that they need to work hard to get ready for the "real world." I

advised you to take internships to get "real world experience." A lot of people

will say that the real world starts once you are out of college; after graduation you become "real adults." "The real world" is intensely attractive to many college students. Most students believe that college is an intermediary stage of being a young adult, rather than a "real adult." A lot of students are eager to graduate and test themselves by "real world" standards, even though they expect the real world to be more demanding than college life. Independence is the main appeal of the real world. We students look forward to time without homework, essays, resident advisors, and time without the authoritarian advice of professors and administrators. In the real world you are finally on your own. At this point many parents decide to "cut-off" their offspring. Most likely, you will no longer be able to depend on other people to pay your bills. The real world is where college students find out if they have learned enough to earn enough to survive outside of the college bubble. The emphasis on independence fits perfectly with broader patterns of American socialization. As Americans, we are taught that growing up means growing apart. We are socialized for autonomy. Our parents applaud our emerging independence and we are congratulated when we can do things on our own. In America, as soon as you are really self-sufficient, you are grown up. So, "the real world" benefits from its association with autonomy, adulthood, and self-reliance. Here in America, unless you are independently wealthy, your independence depends on your income. In order to pay your bills, you need to work. In the real world you are not working for grades, you are working for a living. Failure in the real world is a lot worse than failing an exam in chemistry or economics. Your lifestyle and job both depend on your own ability to provide. For some students, the main attraction of work is the actual work itself. These students feel a calling to serve people and better lives in some capacity. For example, students in medicine, law, or social work look forward to helping to make people better in a better world. On the other hand, for more and more students the attractions of work are mainly monetary. These students do not look to the intrinsic rewards of good work, but to the extrinsic rewards of good pay. Some may just have a desire for an accumulation of money while some look forward to the freedom a high income seemingly promises. Students in college anticipating the freedoms of the real world often forget that this freedom can be quite expensive. Basic, necessary expenses in the real world will include you paying a monthly rent, car payments and insurance, credit card fees, and eating and enjoyment costs. Once you have established a lifestyle, there is more social pressure to upscale than to downshift. American commercial culture works by persuading us to spend money that obligates us to spend more time at work. We often buy entertainment and commodities that have been packaged as an escape from work, hence, expressing a distance and disdain from work. From our working friends on our twitter timelines, how many tweets do we see each Friday saying, "Thank God it's Friday?" When you think about America's social construction of "the real world" we notice the talk basically encases the commercial world – the world of American business. When students talk about "the real world," we are usually not thinking about love and relationships or friends and children. We are not thinking about spiritual life or religious community. We are not even talking about our leisure pursuits, travelling, or vacations. We are talking about the work world; the world where people labor for a wage to support their lifestyle. This world is a dog-eat-dog world, filled with competition and one-upsmanship. By these assumptions we can see how the real world is, in fact, unpleasant and alienating. When students talk about "the real world" we assume it will be hard, tough, and challenging. We know it is not as easy as life in college. Yet, anticipating our impending engagement with reality we seem to take pleasure in its lack of pleasure. We sound like masochists, lusting for pain—"No pain, no gain." Colleges are actual and have a verifiable existence. There are buildings, roads, and parking lots. There are classrooms, dorm rooms, cafeterias and bookstores. Colleges have real income and real expenses. Many people have jobs at colleges. At college people eat, drink, shit and copulate the same way you do in "the real world." So what is the difference from "the real world?" A kiss feels just as good in college as in "the real world"—right? College campuses are not cut off from the world; everyday, resources from all over the world flow in and out of colleges. Yet a college campus is still a bubble. So why do we speak about college as if it were unreal? We define colleges as unreal because students are not paid for schoolwork. As Americans, we tend to believe that if work is not paid then it is not worth much. When we define reality this way, we forget that much of the world's best work is unpaid—like parenting. Yes, let us take a second to appreciate all of our involved mommies and daddies. Even though, some students are in fact paid to think, because they receive grants and scholarships, we do not recognize this as paid work. To some extent, we think colleges are unreal because we view them as a place of preparation. You are not a real doctor until you have completed medical school, passed the Medical College Admission Test (MCAT), and have been certified. Preparation for the real world is a real world activity too. For my fitness freaks, you definitely do not think that food preparation is less real than eating your meal. So why would you think that academic work is less real than paid employment? We define colleges as unreal because of the constant theories and abstract concepts we are always learning about, but never really understanding. We have a predisposition to prefer action, instead of analysis. However, we forget that business also deals with theory, abstractions, and concepts. The standard operation procedures of businesses do not seem theoretical because the theory is already embedded in routines and practices. During you time in college you have become detached from the world and from news about the world. Your day-to-day life as a college student does not give you much time to keep up with what is going on in "the real world"—right? Wrong; you are not as busy as you think, if you want you can stay updated. You believe that once you graduate you will be more in touch because now you are an active member of "the real world." The disconnection you feel is your own choice. You can make time to watch the news, read the newspaper, or use a news application on your phone. On-line news can be superficial so use your judgment on what you actually want to consume. College is generally a space of enough. Students generally have enough food, clothing, and other necessities, but a college campus does not have everything that all different types of individuals may needs. For instance, there are few products and services for woman of color to treat their hair as they would at home, there is a lack of specialized doctors for specific health conditions, and vegans tend to lack the food options they would have outside of a college campus. College is considered unreal because people care about you as a person; college is a place where you build real, meaningful relationships. Some college students find that their professors actually care for them. When we think about the real world and its competitive nature we lose sight of care, cooperation, family, friendship, and church. When "the real world" is broken down into the world of business, it affects both our perception and our experience. Instead of hope, we get diminished expectations and a habit of settling for someone else's understanding of reality. We mock people who see the world through rose-colored glasses, but implicitly praise people who see it cynically in black and white. Even worse, through our conventional definition of the real world, we— the people of higher education—define ourselves as unreal. We deftly define ourselves as unreal and in the process we avoid responsibility for our college lives. If accountability is a feature of "the real world" and we are still in college, we do not have to be accountable. Some students use this as an excuse to maintain their disengagement from the world. It is easier to blame it on the college bubble than to take responsibility for your choices. If the real world is after college, we do not have to think about it nor are we responsible for it. Instead, it is raging time. America's unreal definition of "the real world" has real consequences. It marginalizes values that do not fit the competitive marketplace. It teaches students about the material world and that ideas and idealisms are illusory and ephemeral. Students are taught to believe that interdependence is a fleeting phase of life, and that comprehensive critical thinking is something we will grow out of. In America, and even at American colleges, we worry about the power of ideas and try to avoid them. In high

school, the kid who loves ideas is often marginalized and labeled as the brain,

nerd, or geek. Fortunately, there is more regard for thought and ideas in

college. But, why should this kid have to wait until college? Idealism is the

sense that what should be could be; we have the potential to create a world

we want to live in. Whereas, realism is often the sense that what should be

cannot be; more approaches of skepticism and cynicism. So the social

construction of "the real world" is a way of dismantling our hope. Instead of

learning hoping mechanisms, we content ourselves with coping mechanisms.

We learn to adapt to the demands of our world instead of demanding that the

world adapt to our visions. Too often students prepare themselves to live in

"the real world," instead of the world you really want to live in. We take

courses to fulfill requirements, instead of requiring courses to fulfill us and

help us build a better world. All my talk about "the real world" is merely

words and ideas. But, these words and ideas influence our worlds and ideals.

They inform our hearts and minds, our beliefs and behaviors. So, it is a good

idea to understand the implications of this social construction of "the real

world." The real world is out there, but it is also in here; it is in our hearts,

minds, and souls. "The real world" is not just in the business world; it is in our

families, friendships, and neighborhoods. If we want real world experience, we do not have to get an internship nor live off campus. Education is living life and learning about your mind and ideas. Colleges are a great space to cultivate ideas and design minds. We can begin to realize our ideals in the real world, where we are right now. Education is not preparation for life, cultivating and following your ideals is preparation for your life.

A lot of my Dartmouth classmates may graduate and move off to some fancy high-paying job with flexible hours and lots of vacation days, live in a brand new lofty condo in the best part of town, meet lots of interesting, similar people in a new city and continue to party like they did in college. Unfortunately, for the other majority of non-ivy league graduates their lives may be quite the opposite. After graduation your first and hardest challenge will be finding a job. If you find yourself struggling to find a job, do not take it personally or beat yourself up. The economy is not in its prime and there are countless Americans out of work, so it may not be entirely your fault. Make sure your resume and cover letter are personally tailored to each company you apply to and polish your interviewing skills. Do not think the learning has stopped now that you have graduated. If you are lucky enough to end up at the right job you will probably learn more than you learned in all four years of college. You will be eager to learn and retain information because it will help you in the long run and only benefit your life career. The monetary aspects of "the real world" can be both a nightmare and a celebration. On one hand, you will be forced to make difficult decisions such as health insurance and a retirement plan. Neither of these are very stimulating, nonetheless they are important decision recent grads face in "the real world." On the other hand, the beauty of having a steady job and consistent paycheck is you now have some leeway to spend your money at ease and know that you have another paycheck coming again. Unlike college, you can go spend $100 at the bar and still be able to eat the next day.

Sociology is the scientific study of human societies and social behaviors. Society and the individual are inherently connected, and each depend on one other. How does society affect the individual? How does the individual affect society? The everyday actor in society has the practical knowledge needed to get through daily life. Whereas, a social analyst studies the social world in a consistent, comprehensive, systematic manner. Studying society addresses questions that are seemingly taken for granted wisdom. Sociologists want to cultivate a sociological perspective where people approach the world without preconceptions in order to see things in a new way. One way to gain a sociological perspective is to attempt to create in ourselves a sense of culture shock: a sense of disorientation that occurs when one enters a radically new social or cultural environment. Having the ability to understand the relationship between a particular situation in life and what is happening on a social level deepens your understanding of life. When using a sociological perspective, one focuses on the social context in which people live and how that social context has an impact on individuals' lives. A theory is an abstract proposition that explains the social world and makes predictions about future events. Theories have the ability to change over time because society changes over time.

Throughout our four years in college, students list multiple themes when asked to define success in college. The focus of our success narrative ebbs and flows over time. Making friends is initially important, as students seek to establish a social network in a new environment. Thinking about career-related activities and cementing friendships are more pressing concerns, as students imagine life after college. Conversely, getting good grades is the drumbeat in students' definitions of success. Getting good grades is the most consistently and frequently mentioned theme of defining success in college. Perhaps we are merely responding to an institutional structure that rewards students who academically achieve. Should we change students' desires to get good grades? No. But, can we find ways to encourage them to supplement this with other metrics of success? Yes, by making opportunities for engagement less serendipitous and more deliberate. Highly successful individuals are also highly engaged individuals. A truly successful experience is more than just an impressive transcript. Amidst everything else that goes on during your time in college, it is sometimes easy to lose sight of the end goal: graduation. And when we finally get that diploma in hand, what will it mean? What will we have truly learned and done? Academic success comes in many forms. For most students, it is a stellar transcript that opens doors into great jobs or great graduate schools. For others, academic success also includes what happens outside of the classroom. With so much going on in college, how can you make sure you are headed down a path toward true academic success—and towards a truly rewarding college experience?

There will undoubtedly be a lot of people (including myself) giving you advice about what you should do during and after college. While you may be in school to learn, at some point you will have to make some life decisions. Pick a career and course of study that suits you, not your parents. Learn what you are truly passionate about. Make sure you are happy at your school. Once you have made a choice, feel confident in your decision. Do all you can to learn from the resources around you. Now it is all winding down. You have explored a little, changed your mind here and there, and decided on a major, maybe even a career. With those decisions out of the way, now you can set yourself up for a successful college experience. Make sure you make the most out of the time you have left, be it one year, a couple months, or one week. Take classes from the best professors in different departments. Do not let minor errors in your papers take away from your great ideas. Grab coffee with your favorite professors and talk about what they love about their field. However you spend your time outside of the classroom is a critical part of your college experience. Branch out and try something you have never done before. No matter what you do, make sure you do something that you can look back on and be proud of. College can be overwhelming. So remember to, take care of all of yourself, not just that big brain of yours.

In our modern day there is a strong tendency to value things in merely measurable terms: prices, costs, and paychecks. Therefore, if college is viewed simply by maximizing the future income, then of course it would make sense to reason and take account of what careers and majors are likely to pay the most after graduation. While information like this is important, it needs to be contextualized and not become all-determining. A paycheck is not a statement about your inherent value as a person. The size of your paycheck does communicate something; it represents that value that your work has in the marketplace, a value set either by political decree or voluntary cooperation.

Reliability is provided from the compensation a person receives being a judgment about that person's fulfillment of some kind of demand. For instance, when boxer, Floyd Mayweather, gets a guaranteed payout of $40 million to fight on a pay-per-view event, it tell us something about the willingness of large numbers of people to pay around $70 to see him fight on television or upwards of $2,000 to see the fight live. Still, the size of Maywheather's paycheck does not say anything about the moral status of boxing. Just because someone is willing to compensate you, even significantly, to do something does not mean that it defines your values. Some of the most lucrative jobs are those which are inherently immoral or even illegal.

Chapter 7- Success in "The Real World"

We have all heard stories of internet billionaires, wealthy young actors, and other tales of spectacular overnight success. Knowing how well other people have done in business and how quickly they experienced a major life change can be demotivating. It can make young people lose confidence and feel as if they do not want to get started on something unless it is going to be the next hit. This gives us young people a self-defeating mentality. Combat it by reminding yourself that you are not competing against anyone but yourself. When putting together my business plan and getting advice from entrepreneurial mentors I learned that the important thing is to get your feet wet, not take over the business world. Regardless of how organized and enthusiastic you are, some days will overwhelm you. Do not be afraid to step back from work and do whatever relaxes you. If you love the endorphin rush of exercise, then exercise. If you love the company of friends, go hang out with your friends. Or, if you love the peace and solitude of meditation, go meditate. When you start to feel overwhelmed close your eyes, take a breath, and remember pain is temporary. Take advantage of opportunities to invigorate yourself and balance your responsibilities with relaxation. Our generation of twenty-something year olds have a real complex to address and conquer: we all want the frills of a successful career, yet are not willing to put in the work needed to earn them. We just do not want to pay our dues anymore. Some of us grew up being coddled by our parents or receiving praise, trophies or accolades for half-ass work. The idea that you might actually have to work hard in order to earn success has gotten lost in the new millennial. Nowadays lifestyle analysts ignore the idea of hard work with the attitude that paying your dues is an outdated idea.

Remember all those labor laws we learned in social studies? Well as an intern you can forget all about them. Many interns will work for long periods of time in an unpaid position in order to build their resumes and work experience. Therefore, we can note that there is an economical class difference between those who can afford to work for free and those who cannot. The reality is that interns perform many important day to day corporate operations, especially the very monotonous work. If you have the option and financial stability to intern abroad, do it. When you intern abroad you will receive a lot of the same benefits as studying abroad. You will be immersed in a new culture and get the chance to learn firsthand about the different customs. Interning abroad can provide useful global relationships, connections, and networks that can help you professionally. You will be able to develop a global perspective and understanding, which is extremely helpful in today's globalized economy.

Above all, interning abroad will build your resume, build your work experience, and make you stand out amongst the competition.

Here is where we deconstruct the definition of paying your dues; Paying your dues means putting in the time and work to attain your dream career. You have to start somewhere and understand that you may not be compensated in the beginning. I have people very close to me that would rather live unemployed at home with their parents because they refuse to take a "menial" job that they feel is beneath them. You have to start at the bottom of the food chain if you want to move up the corporate ladder. Is it not obvious that you need to get experience and learn the trade and skills? This takes time. During an interview I was asked how much experience and knowledge I had on commercial real estate in New York City, I said very little but that I am a quick learner. The Chief Operating Officer very quickly told me that the learning curve is fifteen years. Success comes from years of hard work. I do not know of any magic pill to take or special button to press to become instantly successful. Dedicate time to mastering your skills. You must put in countless hours of mastering your subject, defer parties, and spend sleepless nights working on business plans or portfolios. I know it is possible to become wealthy early in life if you have the drive, determination, and ambition to succeed. Also, when you first get into the working world do not expect to live the same lifestyle you had when you were at home being supported by your parents. The fancy clothes, nice furniture, new car, and spacious house are a lot less common when you have to pay for them on your own. Let patience and perseverance become your best friends along your path towards a successful career. I know it seems like there are all these get-rich-quick schemes and overnight internet millionaires, but those successes actually come from years of hard work. Take Facebook for example. Harvard student Mark Zuckerberg started Facebook in 2004 and now it has become one of the most trafficked sites on the internet. But, Zuckerberg started programming in middle school. In college Zuckerberg polished the knowledge and skills necessary to build Facebook. Even after Facebook was launched it still took a few years for the site to grow to the where it is today. We would all love to get rich in a day, but unless you win the lottery, it most likely just is not in the cards for you. I understand the desire and importance of our generation to work less and have more time for living, enjoying life, hence the importance of balance. Allotted time spent working has to be smart, productive, and efficient. You can have a successful career and not be slave to your work, but first you have to pay your dues to be in this position. Be willing to make short-term sacrifices for long-term goals. Be willing to pay your dues early on (in order to reap rewards late). Be willing to manage your time gaining the skills and putting in the work to make your dream a reality.

You might find yourself saying yes to things that you do not even care about and no to things that could make your life better in some way. For example, when you say yes to happy hour, you are actually saying no to a workout of your choice. When you say yes to watching pointless reality television shows, you are really saying no to getting the sleep your body needs. It could be you do not need to entirely quit saying yes. Instead, you may just need to acknowledge when you are saying yes and what you are trading for it. At some point in your career, you inevitably are going to find out what people do not like about your approach, product, or service. Bad news is bad news. Do not ignore your senses or negative critic. You should always want to find the bad news out as early as possible, to keep your losses to a minimum. Successful people work with what they have at hand and whatever comes there way. Successful people try to use everything at their disposal in achieving their goals; This is why they are grateful for surprises, obstacles, and even disappointments. It gives them more information and resources to draw upon. This helps keep them ahead of the other person and improves their odds of being successful. If you have a different mindset, you will have a different outcome. If you make different choices from your peers, then your life will be different from your peers. As a young worker, most people will see your age as your biggest hurdle and most pressing hindrance. Truth is, your youth might be your biggest advantage. Some older employers look for someone hungry and motivated, but also, someone who has grown up around technology. There is definitely a perceived disadvantage to being a young "inexperienced" worker or entrepreneur. But, being young does not mean you do not know what you are doing or that you have not put in the time and energy to become an expert in your field. As a young job seeker or entrepreneur, your network is key. "You are who your friends are." We will often emulate the people we are closest to and, if those people are successful, your own chances of success rise in proportion. If your three closest friends are highly motivated and successful individuals, these traits will likely spur you to work even harder. In my own experience, spending time with successful people has allowed me to meet interesting individuals and expand my professional network. The relationships I have fostered have been sincere. A big part of my current social life is surrounding myself with successful people who understand what I am working toward and can even be of assistance to helping me reach my goals. Connecting with the right ambitious young people is extremely effective for allowing you to see what direction your own path to success might take. There is nothing holding you back from being successful at a young age. You just need to work hard, have confidence in your abilities, and surround yourself with positive and successful people. For entry-level positions your major will be of more importance. Having the suggested major listed on the job posting is clearly more relevant and one of the top criteria employers are looking for. If your major or background is not listed as the preferred credentials for a position you can still make it clear that you have the skills required to do the job well. If your major seems unconventional in light of the job you are applying for, use your cover letter to highlight the relevant skills you learned that the hiring manager might be surprised by. Later on in your career your progression and experience is more important. After a certain period of time employers will be less likely to care about your undergraduate major. Employers like to see a history of high achievement. If you have gone to a great school, expressed leadership qualities, and achieved a high grade point average, employers will favor these over a particular major. If you have skills that are in demand, you are set. If you are applying to an engineering job or a computer science job, of course the corresponding major is going to have the competitive edge. But, there is such a demand right now for good programmers and technologists that if you were able to teach yourself programming languages and demonstrate them on a skills test or through a portfolio of work, you would still stand a high chance at getting hired, even if you majored in something less relevant. In other industries and positions your major may be less important. A liberal arts degree can be applicable for a variety of jobs. One aspect you will want to stress is how your particular major taught you advantageous critical thinking and problem solving skills. If you think about all the information on your resume—your relevant work, internships, externships, extracurricular activities, school reputation, family ties, volunteer work, and GPA—your major is just one point. Your main objective should be to achieve and in-person interview. Use this interview as an opportunity to display your assets, talents, and skills. If you do this successfully, your major will matter less. Creativity, adaptability, time management, and communications are essential skills hiring agent look for in recent college graduates. How are you going to prove you have the skills they are looking for? You could be the best candidate for your dream job and they might never know—so, be smart and devise your plan of attack. Show them that you have the skills needed to succeed in a fast-changing workplace. Still, be realistic and know how constructive and valuable majors are towards your career training.

Chapter 8- Does it all really matter?

We ponder the successes, failures, and standout events that are slowly narrating our life's story. Reflection is the key to progression. This process of self-reflection helps us maintain a conscious awareness of where we have been and where we intend to go. Self-reflection is pertinent to the organization and preservation of our dreams, goals, and desires. In "the real world" we spend our time thinking about money, and how much money shapes the way we interact in the world. We think that we need that pleasure, car, woman, man, house, dress, and bank balance in order to be okay, happy, and feel complete. We think this because we are socialized to think it. Bad news.... we are wrong. We do not need any monetary gain, power, or person to be happy; as I learned in my Native American studies' class, we need to relinquish the sense of need itself. When you get what you want, you stop wanting. So, what you really want is to not want. So why not cut out the interim phase and just stop wanting those things in the first place? Do not be scared of the real world. You will make lifelong friends, you will continue learning, and you will not need to supply an excuse when you want to go to bed early. You will navigate this stage the same way you did all the others: with resourcefulness, fear, and alcohol. For those of you not ready for the real world you may end up delaying the real world. For some this is a great

opportunity to seek out adventure and travel as an alternative—lucky you!

When you step back and ask "who am I?" what answers

do you get? The self is self-created. The process of building a self is a

creative act. Your life has only one author, and its main character only has one

source. Even if you blame the outside world or certain circumstances for your

problems or wish you had a missing X factor: more money, an Ivy League

degree, or better parents, these thoughts also become part of your story. No

one is exempt from this truth. The you that has the greatest chance for success

is driven by higher aspirations. The you that has no aspirations is very likely

to fall short. You with aspirations is: curious, open-minded, and eager for new

experiences, finds motivation from within, wants to be self-sufficient but does

not have to be, speaks your own truth, has inspiring role models, and feels

attached to a higher purpose. While the you with no aspirations: fears loss and

allows fear to stand in the way of boundless opportunities, is greedy for gain,

measures yourself by external rewards (money, power, status, possessions), is

reluctant to trust, takes a defensive and self-protective stance, has no higher

values except self-interest. There is a great deal of social pressure and social acceptance to think that the you without aspirations is more desirable than the you with aspirations. Falsely, we often see the stance of winners defined by overachieving, ruthless competitors. If you do not defend your self-interest, who will? If you place your trust and genuine concern in others you will find that there are people out there wanting to protect your self-interest too. Does anyone want to be idealistic, "soft", or compliant? If you answer no, you are letting externals define your attitude, because there is nothing soft about having aspirations.

Sometimes a reality check is just an occasion when we tell the truth to ourselves. In other situations it is a way of avoiding the truth about reality. A reality check asks us to examine our assumptions, and to identify the illusions that we may not even see are causing us grief. We might aspire to be a professional basketball player; a reality check reminds us that we are not that talented. We might hope to be a straight A student; a reality check notifies us that we are not that smart. We may want to be exceptionally buff and muscular; a reality check would remind us that we just do not have the body for that. Usually, a reality check asks us to keep our aspirations in line with our actual abilities, so that we are not continuously disappointed. It does not ask us to give up hope. Instead, a reality check keeps us from wishful thinking.

Remember, we never want to rely of wishes and luck to lead us to success. While phrases like "get real" may be the voice of practical pessimism that reinforces the standard vision of "the real world," we can still adjust to the cynicism of the real world. The actual realist are America's idealists; people who understand both the needs of human nature and the needs of the world. Capitalism has been a catalyst for human imagination and inventiveness, but in modern time the destruction seems to be outpacing the creativity. In the United States we have major issues of homelessness, inequalities of pay, low birth-weight babies, poverty, and credit harms, yet seem to focus more on big homes, executive salaries, and private consumption. If we performed a reality check on "the real world" we would see that it does not encompass the whole world. Environmentally, "the real world" is a disaster. Our conventional definition of the real world omits many of the real world wonders and pleasures of the people and places that surround us. So, if we realized all the implications of our social construction of "the real world," we would realize alternative visions of reality. We do not just go into a real world that is already made. We make the real world in our everyday lives. We make it by our beliefs and behaviors, by the way we act, and by the way we speak. Therefore, we need to be conscience of the decisions we are making and why we are making those decisions. If we continue to talk about "the real world" as if it were somewhere else, we are likely to miss the real world all around us. If we continue to prepare to go out into "the real world," we will be unprepared to affect the real world we inhabit now. When we act on our ideals, we make them real. As we learn what defines the world around us, we can make a real world that is really worth living in. Youth can be your biggest assist. Nevertheless, the problem is how do you overcome the preconceived notions that come with being a younger professional? People will argue that your youth means you are inexperienced, naïve, and in for a rude awakening. Prove your skeptics wrong by showing your critics how youthful characteristics like curiosity and optimism are great keys to succeed. Young people have the ability to learn new skills quickly and retain a lot of information at one time. Imagine your parents trying to learn a new language, as opposed to you taking a two term Portuguese class and becoming proficient. Those experienced in a specific field become jaded, whereas young people do not see any boundaries and can adapt to an evolving industry quickly. In this case, being completely unaware of what lies ahead of you is beneficial and young people hold that upper hand. Trust your instincts, because your natural intuition will shape the vision and execution of the business or organization you are trying to build. Deviating from your instincts will bring unrest for you and your stakeholders, making you wish you had gone with your instincts in the first place. Capitalize on your youth. Test your curiosity, limits, and capacity. Stretch your mind and your physical capabilities to the maximum without consequences. Do not be shy around the older professionals and do not hide your ideas. Instead, let them flow and mingle amongst the others. Continue being innovative. To our benefit, adults tend to expect less from young people. Use this to your advantage because it is easier to exceed expectations and harder to not meet them. Your creativity is most likely at a high point. Younger generations have a fresh perspective on the world because we are immersed in the new technologies. This perspective lends itself to seeing many opportunities that have not already been exploited. Sadly, many people under-estimate young employees. But there are many strengths to being young. You have more energy. You are in your prime health when you are somewhere in your twenties. Being young and having more energy is one of the many reasons people want to have children at a young age. Having more energy than the older employees gives you a potential advantage for increased efficiency or the ability to work longer hours without complaining. Being young gives you an edge. Young people are flexible. Most young people do not have long-term relationships or significant ties. This is valuable in the workplace where a young person has the ability to pack his or her bags and move for a better position much easier than an older, settled down employee. Also, younger employees have more flexibility to work nights and weekends when needed. Even if you are in a committed relationship, you may still have more flexibility than those with kids. Since our generation grew up surrounded by technology, it is easier for us to understand and navigate some of the more complicated programs without official training. With the increasing use of technology we will continue being profitable in the professional world. Young adults are increasingly busy between school work, job work, or socializing. Therefore, we know how to multitask and prioritize to make things more efficient. I have a personal lust for multitasking; Multitasking drives me to find the most efficient ways to do things and not waste time. So, who would you rather draft for your NBA roster? The young person who is going to do things without asking why or someone who is going to do things faster and more efficient. Having the strengths in our arsenal tank is definitely advantageous, but if we do not display them then they mean absolutely nothing. In order to be successful in your career as a young person, you have to learn the best way to display your strengths. Coming across too strong or egotistical can rub people the wrong way and lead them to ignore everything positive about you. On the other hand, not taking any initiative can leave you left in a cubicle for the rest of your life. When tasks are assigned to you, be intentional about producing top quality work. You should want to produce quality work consistently.

Never turn in something you know is poor quality. You name will be associated with this and your reputation goes a long way when it comes to future job opportunities. Be willing to take on new tasks. When new projects come up that you can handle, volunteer to be a part of it. Supervisors want to have team players working for them, so show them how much of a team player you are. Be social in your workplace, but do not allow it to take you away from your work. Let your coworkers and supervisors get to know you. Do not try and impress them—this is not junior high anymore. Simply be yourself and be kind to those you work with. Times are changing and opportunities are rising for people who show the initiative and skills to succeed. Do not let the culture of disrespect and hazing for young adults hold you back. Instead, use this as motivation to prove them wrong and display your success. Stay focused on the long term goal you have planned. It can be easy to get sidetracked and feel comfortable in a position. Thinking long term is a great way to keep your focus and prevent yourself from settling for being average. When coworkers get fired up into a negative train of conversation find a diplomatic way to either remove yourself or change the topic. Following the whiners by negatively partaking in the conversation is only counter-productive to your success.

Chapter 9- I know living happy matters

It is important to question "What are people for?" because if you do not, you might settle for a mediocre existence. It is important to ask "What are my deepest values?" because if you do not, you might live a life you do not really value. It is important to ask "Why do we act the way we do?" because otherwise you might never get wise to the ways of your culture. It is a necessity to ask big questions, even if you cannot always find the big answers. It is easy to get caught up in our own lives and forget what makes life so amazing in the first place. When I get like this I like to remind myself of a few realizations:

You can smile today

You can better yourself every day

You five years ago has nothing on you today

You have the potential to make someone smile

You have gotten through so many times when you thought you couldn't

You can ask the questions that other people don't

You can learn something new about yourself

You can believe anything you want to

You are alive today

Learn about yourself. Find out how your mind, body, and soul work separately and in unison. The key to reducing stress in your life is to find the root of the problem. What leads you to being stressed? Whether it is a relationship in your life, school, a job, try to figure out the cause. Once you identify the cause, it will become easier to be proactive about countering the stress or anxiety. Write down a list of the aspects of your life that consistently stress you out. Order the list from most stressful to least stressful. Recognizing the cause and writing down your problems will make it much easier to conquer. Giving is dually good for you and good for the people or persons you are giving to. Giving to others activates areas of the brain linked to pleasure, trust, and social connection. Giving releases endorphins that boost happiness for both us and the people we help. Remember that feeling of happiness you felt buying your mom or significant other or friend that awesome Christmas gift? Giving connects us to others, creates stronger communities, and helps build a happier environment for everyone. You do not necessarily have to give money; you can give your time, ideas, knowledge, care and energy. You can help family, friends, neighbors, or even strangers—no need to be rich. If you are skeptical of this giving concept, start small. Give a smile, a kind word, or a thoughtful gesture. Kindness and caring are really key to creating trusting relationships. In the real estate world, remembering a simple fact about a potential client, like a family member's name, can create business opportunities. Because, human beings value care and kindness. You might not realize or be entirely aware of how important your relationships with others are towards your wellbeing and happiness. Even so, real relationships matter because our connections with other people are at the heart of our happiness. If you have poor relationships with your family, friends, colleagues, or neighbors you most likely have a disheartened mental health. Not having close personal ties poses the same level of health risks as smoking or obesity. Having high levels of social support and social connections betters your health and appears to increase your overall immune system, reducing physical and mental decline as we age. Close, secure, and supportive relationships allow you to experience positive emotions together, talk openly, feel understood, give and receive support, and share in activities and experiences. Relationships will make you happier and happy people tend to have better quality relationships. We are social creatures that naturally survive and evolve on relationships. Forgo your Darwinism theories of survival of your own genes, because it is the survival of the group that is most likely to be most successful. We need to love, be loved, care, and be cared for. So, instead of ignoring your human nature look for opportunities to strengthen your relationships with others and your encompassing happiness. Know that by doing this for yourself, your happiness will be contagious across your broader social networks— enabling your communities to flourish. Support is not just there for when times are tough. Sharing good news is also a main principal for building our relationships and increasing happiness. Find a balance between work, relationships, family, and your social life. Taking care of our bodies and minds are not only connected, but also a necessity. Being active is undoubtedly good for our physical health. Also, being active instantly improves our mood and can even lift us out of a depression. I have a friend who was self-medicating with non-prescribed Adderall and Xanax. She was always tired, always out of it, never herself, and facing a downhill depression. Until, one weekend we took a mini-vacation to our friend's Pennsylvania house where we forced her to go hiking, walk trails, and just be active. It was clear that this was a turning point for her. She said she "felt alive" for the first time in a while and no longer wanted to miss out on actually feeling emotions. She did not need to run a marathon or turn into a professional athlete overnight. There are simple things we can all do to be more active each day. Unplug from your everyday use of technology and go outside. But, most importantly do not forget the importance of sleep. Make sure you get enough sleep for your body to function at its best. There are times when we need the time to unwind, decompress, and simply chill. Life can come at all of us hard and fast. As time keeps going forward at its own natural pace, not always the pace we would choose, you may start to feel overwhelmed. Fatigue, stress, and exhaustion may hit you faster than you think or even notice. The best remedy for this is rest; do not ignore your body's need to rest. Stop and take notice of the things right in front of you. Time dedicated to appreciating is time spent living. Learning to be more mindful and aware helps us get in tune with our feelings and stops us from dwelling on the past or worrying about the future. Do you not want to get the most out of every day which you are currently living? Taking notice of the things right in front of us requires mindfulness; being intentional, attentive, aware and accepting, instead of judging. The hardest part I have had with being mindful of my surroundings is not overthinking. Taking notice and being mindful means that you are observing, but not getting caught up in thinking and worrying about what it is that you are seeing. By mastering this we gain control over what we decide to give our attention to. In today's busy, multi-tasking world, few of us naturally are mindful, still it is something we can learn and benefit from. It is seemingly simple, but takes practice. To notice the moments around you means to live in the moment. When we savor every moment, we are savoring the happy moments of our lives. Learning influences our well-being in various positive ways. Learning exposes us to new ideas that help us stay curious and engaged. Learning also provides a sense of accomplishment which facilitates boosting our self-confidence and resilience. You can learn new things through formal schooling or informal methods of education. Future goals motivate us, challenge us, and excite us. Feeling good about the future is important to our happiness. Having unattainable goals brings about unnecessary stress, meanwhile having challenging yet achievable goals excites us. Choosing ambitious, but realistic goals gives our lives a sense of direction and satisfaction that we can achieve them. Goals are part of the foundation for turning our values and dreams into reality. Happiness is not formed overnight, it comes from thinking, planning, and pursuing the things we deem important to us. Look inward for your goals— do not rely on other people's goals or what others want for you. Because, goals are most successful when they are something we honestly want to achieve and have been set for ourselves. Goals may vary in time, still all goals are significant. A long-term goal might be your life goal, your desired career, or to obtain a qualification. While, a short-term goal might be to organize an upcoming event, save a certain amount of money, or lose a certain amount of weight. People see smaller goals as being less important, but having personal, smaller projects that matter to us and are attainable will boost your well-being. The way we set goals, the actions we take to achieve them, and the energy and effort we put in matter. Some of our goals may seem ambitious, but can still be achievable. Be that as it may, good goal-setting can be learned. The absence of goals in our lives or avoiding to pursue our goals makes us feel like we are stuck and ineffective. Taking an optimistic approach to our goals necessitates: choosing goals that take us towards something positive we want to accomplish, rather than choosing goals that help us avoid things we do not want, being proactive when issues arise and looking for ways to resolve them, rather than ignoring or delaying them, and avoiding constant reflection on the negative, instead, learning to accept difficult things that we cannot change and re-adjusting. An overly optimistic outlook will be unhelpful if you blindly ignore the facts. But, having a realistic and hopeful view of the outcomes can increase your likelihood of success and happiness. Be an optimist who learns how to cope better, seeks support from others rather than withdraws from those around you, who does not ignore the difficulties of life, but takes them head on. Known when enough is enough. What gives you joy and happiness the first time may not work the second time. Set healthy and reasonable boundaries for yourself and do not overdo it. Joy, gratitude, pride, inspiration, pleasure, and humor are positive emotions that we should regularly experience. Skeptics will say that these emotions are good to have, but not vital for our survival as negative emotions are. Being as relationships are vital to our

survival, and positive emotions help us build the resources that lead to

successful relationships, I would argue that positive emotions are equally (if

not more than) important to our survival. The balance between positive and

negative emotions is essential. Find your balance between feeling deflated in

the short term and finding activities that bring greater happiness in the long

run. My old basketball coach used to tell our team how our thoughts become

words, our words become our actions and our actions define who we are. If

you want to have a positive day, you need to start the day with a positive

mindset. Being alive and healthy is a privilege—a privilege not everyone gets

to enjoy. Once you start seeing your life as a blessing, it will start to feel like

one. All of us face our times of stress, trauma, loss, or failure in our lives. But

how we respond to these is what impacts our welfare. Resilience can be

learned. Being able to bounce back and cope with adversity will benefit you

along your path of success and happiness. Having the capability to persevere

and adapt when faced with challenges are some key characteristics of

successful people. Being flexible enough to bend instead of break when faced

with pressure will make you more open and willing to take on new

opportunities. All of us can benefit from increasing our resilience. By building

a range of skills and resources to help us respond flexibly and effectively to challenges we can recover quickly and learn and grow as an individual along the way. Yes, we have already experienced some adversity during our lives that has already increased our adversity, but we can continue to build our resilience skills. By changing the way we think about adversity we can boost how resilient we are. Finding a way to put an adverse situation in perspective makes you think of those in worse situations and enables you to make sense of your situation. Finding some benefit that has come as a result of the difficulty can be constructive. Then, we can pay attention to our coping skills and resources used. Remember, it is not about denial, rather trying to find the good in the bad. Experiences that bring us face to face with the fragility of life sharpen our appreciation of life. How many times have you heard "No-one is perfect?" Do you believe it yet? If not, well now it is time you change that. Again, no-one is perfect. Stop comparing your insides to other people's outsides. Learn to accept yourself and be kinder to yourself when things go wrong. This will increase your resilience, level of enjoyment in life, and mental and physical health. This will be an ongoing effect that will help you accept others as they are. Self-acceptance will allow you to work on the things you do not do well or mistakes you have made, rather than having those mistakes work against you. Teach yourself to be comfortable with the person that you are. We all want to live happy, successful, and fulfilling lives and I hope we all want the people we love to be happy too. Therefore, happiness matters to all of us. Happiness includes our internal feelings and attitudes as well as our external circumstances like, health, occupation, financial situations. However, happiness and fulfillment come less from material wealth and more from relationships. Make peace with your past. Our relationship with ourselves is first and foremost, then our relationships with those important to us, and those we interact with and make up society with.

People have a tendency to confuse success and happiness. We live in a culture based on profit and earning and we have grown to attribute happiness as the product of success. Equating success to the forefront of happiness is wrong and may lead you down a road of regret. We are all aware that the most successful and rich people are not always the happiest. Many of these successful people will tell you stories of how they opted to give up their chances for happiness on their way to the top. Happiness should be your main focused, overall life achievement, while success is a singular accomplishment. Hence, success should come as a byproduct of happiness. If you follow this rule of thumb, happiness will still be present even when success is gone. Happiness is not impossible without the perfect career. Sometimes a job simply earns money so that other time can be spent on the things that really make us happy. Define success in inner terms. In a society propelled by advertising, mass media, competition, and dynamic chance, the temptation to run with the majority of society is strong, and the majority is always running towards external rewards. A you without aspirations will never be in a position to fully experience the possibilities that are hidden within.

Only fools use their mouth to speak. A smart person uses his or her brain, and a wise person uses his or her heart.

Find Out More About The Author,

Kamala Thompson

Email: KamalaThompson@NewEraPlanning.com

Website: www.NewEraPlanning.com

Twitter: @ThompsonKamala

Instagram: New_Era_Planning

Phone: 631.413.0621

Made in the USA
Charleston, SC
31 July 2014